First Workshop on Federated Learning for Natural Language Processing (FL4NLP 2022)

Dublin, Ireland
27 May 2022

ISBN: 978-1-7138-6738-8

Printed from e-media with permission by:

Curran Associates, Inc.
57 Morehouse Lane
Red Hook, NY 12571

Some format issues inherent in the e-media version may also appear in this print version.

Printed with permission by Curran Associates, Inc. (2023)

Association for Computational Linguistics
209 N. Eighth Street
Stroudsburg, Pennsylvania 18360

Phone: 1-570-476-8006
Fax: 1-570-476-0860

acl@aclweb.org

Additional copies of this publication are available from:

Curran Associates, Inc.
57 Morehouse Lane
Red Hook, NY 12571 USA
Phone: 845-758-0400
Fax: 845-758-2633
Email: curran@proceedings.com
Web: www.proceedings.com

FL4NLP 2022

The First Workshop on Federated Learning for Natural Language Processing

Proceedings of the Workshop

May 27, 2022

The FL4NLP organizers gratefully acknowledge the support from the following sponsors.

Gold

FedML

intel labs

amazon alexa

Introduction

Due to increasing concerns and regulations about data privacy (e.g., General Data Protection Regulation), coupled with the growing computational power of edge devices, emerging data from realistic users have become much more fragmented, forming distributed private datasets across different clients (i.e., organizations or personal devices). Respecting users' privacy and restricted by these regulations, we have to assume that users' data in a client are not allowed to transfer to a centralized server or other clients. For example, a hospital does not want to share its private data (e.g., conversations, questions asked on its website/app) with other hospitals. This is despite the fact that models trained by a centralized dataset (i.e., combining data from all clients) usually enjoy better performance on downstream tasks (e.g., dialogue, question answering). Therefore, it is of vital importance to study NLP problems in such a scenario, where data are distributed across different isolated organizations or remote devices and cannot be shared for privacy concerns.

The field of federated learning (FL) aims to enable many individual clients to jointly train their models, while keeping their local data decentralized and completely private from other users or a centralized server. A common training schema of FL methods is that each client sends its model parameters to the server, which updates and sends back the global model to all clients in each round. Since the raw data of one client has never been exposed to others, FL is promising to be an effective way to address the above challenges, particularly in the NLP domain where many user-generated text data contain sensitive, personal information.

Our workshop website is `https://fl4nlp.github.io/`.

Organizing Committee

Organizing Committee

Bill Yuchen Lin, University of Southern California
Chaoyang He, University of Southern California
Chulin Xie, University of Illinois Urbana-Champaign
Fatemehsadat Mireshghallah, University of California San Diego
Ninareh Mehrabi, University of Southern California
Tian Li, Carnegie Mellon University
Mahdi Soltanolkotabi, University of Southern California
Xiang Ren, University of Southern California

Program Committee

Program Chairs

Bill Yuchen Lin, University of Southern California
Chaoyang He, University of Southern California
Tian Li, Carnegie Mellon University
Ninareh Mehrabi, University of Southern California
Fatemehsadat Mireshghallah, University of California, San Diego
Xiang Ren, University of Southern California
Mahdi Soltanolkotabi, University of Southern California
Chulin Xie, University of Illinois, Urbana Champaign

Program Committee

Hongyuan Zhan
Anit Kumar Sahu
Bahareh Harandizadeh
Basak Guler
Dimitris Stripelis
Eugene Bagdasaryan
Farzin Haddadpour
Gerald Penn
Hongyi Wang
Jinhyun So
Jun Yan
Kshitiz Malik
Kevin Hsieh
Ninareh Mehrabi
Roozbeh Yousefzadeh
Saurav Prakash
Shen Li
Shengyuan Hu
Sijie Cheng
Sunwoo Lee
Tao Yu
Umang Gupta
Xin Dong
Xuechen Li
Yae Jee Cho
Zheng Xu

Invited Speakers

Salman Avestimehr, University of Southern California
Virginia Smith, CMU
Bo Li, UIUC
Tong Zhang, HKUST
Manzil Zaheer, Google DeepMind

Rahul Gupta, Amazon Alexa

Table of Contents

ActPerFL: Active Personalized Federated Learning
Huili Chen, Jie Ding, Eric William Tramel, Shuang Wu, Anit Kumar Sahu, Salman Avestimehr and Tao Zhang 1

Scaling Language Model Size in Cross-Device Federated Learning
Jae Hun Ro, Theresa Breiner, Lara McConnaughey, Mingqing Chen, Ananda Theertha Suresh, Shankar Kumar and Rajiv Mathews 6

Adaptive Differential Privacy for Language Model Training
Xinwei Wu, li Gong and Deyi Xiong 21

Intrinsic Gradient Compression for Scalable and Efficient Federated Learning
Luke Melas-Kyriazi and Franklyn Wang 27

Program

Friday, May 27, 2022

09:00 - 09:10	*Opening Remarks*
09:10 - 10:05	*Invited Speaker 1*
10:05 - 11:00	*Invited Speaker 2*
11:05 - 12:00	*Invited Speaker 3*
12:00 - 12:30	*Lunch Break*
12:35 - 12:50	*Paper Presentation 1*
12:50 - 13:05	*Paper Presentation 2*
13:05 - 13:20	*Paper Presentation 3*
13:20 - 13:35	*Paper Presentation 4*
13:35 - 14:30	*Invited Speaker 4*
14:30 - 15:25	*Invited Speaker 5*
15:25 - 16:20	*Invited Speaker 6*
16:20 - 16:35	*Paper Presentation 5*
16:35 - 16:50	*Paper Presentation 6*
16:50 - 17:05	*Paper Presentation 7*
17:05 - 17:20	*Paper Presentation 8*
17:20 - 17:35	*Paper Presentation 9*
17:35 - 18:30	*Panel Discussion (TBA)*

Friday, May 27, 2022 (continued)

18:40 - 18:30 *Closing Remarks*

ActPerFL: Active Personalized Federated Learning

Huili Chen, Jie Ding, Eric Tramel, Shuang Wu,
Anit Kumar Sahu, Salman Avestimehr, Tao Zhang
Alexa AI, Amazon
{chehuili,jiedi,eritrame,wushuan,anitsah,avestime,taozhng}@amazon.com

Abstract

In the context of personalized federated learning (FL), the critical challenge is to balance local model improvement and global model tuning when the personal and global objectives may not be exactly aligned. Inspired by Bayesian hierarchical models, we develop ActPerFL, a self-aware personalized FL method where each client can automatically balance the training of its local personal model and the global model that implicitly contributes to other clients' training. Such a balance is derived from the *inter-client and intra-client uncertainty quantification*. Consequently, ActPerFL can adapt to the underlying clients' heterogeneity with *uncertainty-driven local training and model aggregation.* With experimental studies on Sent140 and Amazon Alexa audio data, we show that ActPerFL can achieve superior personalization performance compared with the existing counterparts.

1 Introduction

Federated learning (FL) (Konevcny et al., 2016; McMahan et al., 2017) is transforming machine learning (ML) ecosystems from "centralized in-the-cloud" to "distributed across-clients," to potentially leverage the computation and data resources of billions of edge devices (Lim et al., 2020), without raw data leaving the devices. As a distributed ML framework, FL aims to train a global model that aggregates gradients or model updates from the participating edge devices. Recent research in FL has significantly extended its original scope to address the emerging concern of personalization, a broad term that often refers to an FL system that accommodates client-specific data distributions of interest (Dinh et al., 2020a; Fallah et al., 2020a).

In particular, each client in a personalized FL system holds data that can be potentially non-IID. For example, smart edge devices at different houses may collect audio data of heterogeneous nature (Purington et al., 2017; Diao et al., 2020, 2021) due to, e.g., accents, background noises, and house structures. Each device hopes to improve its on-device model through personalized FL without transmitting sensitive data. While the practical benefits of personalization have been widely acknowledged, its theoretical understanding remains unclear. Existing works on personalized FL often derive algorithms based on a pre-specified optimization formulation or model aggregation rule.

In this work, we start with a toy example and develop insights into the nature of personalization from a statistical uncertainty perspective. In particular, we aim to answer the following critical questions regarding personalized FL.

(Q1) The lower-bound baselines of personalized FL can be obtained in two cases, i.e., each client performs local training without FL, or all clients participate in conventional FL training. However, the upper-bound for the client is unclear.

(Q2) Suppose that the goal of each client is to improve its local model performance. How to design an FL training that interpret the global model, suitably aggregate local models and fine-tune each client's local training automatically?

Both questions are challenging. The question (Q1) demands a systematic way to characterize the client-specific and globally-shared information. To this end, we draw insights from a simplified and analytically tractable setting: *two-level Bayesian hierarchical models*, where the two levels respectively describe inter-client and intra-client uncertainty.

We make the following technical contributions:

- Interpreting personalization from a *hierarchical model-based* perspective and providing theoretical analyses for FL training.
- Proposing ActPerFL, an active personalized FL solution that guides local training and global aggregation via inter- and intra-client *uncertainty quantification.*
- Presenting a novel implementation of ActPerFL for deep learning, consisting of auto-

Proceedings of the First Workshop on Federated Learning for Natural Language Processing (FL4NLP 2022), pages 1 - 5
May 27, 2022 ©2022 Association for Computational Linguistics

mated hyper-parameter tuning for clients and an adaptive aggregation rule.

- Evaluating ActPerFL on Sent140 and Amazon Alexa audio data. Empirical results show promising personalization performance compared with existing methods.

To our best knowledge, ActPerFL is the first work that utilizes uncertainty quantification to drive FL personalization.

2 Bayesian View of Personalized FL

We discuss how ActPerFL approaches personalized FL with theoretical insights from the Bayesian perspective in this section. To develop insights, we study a two-level Gaussian model. Similar arguments can be derived for generic parametric models. The notations are defined as follows. Let $\mathcal{N}(\mu, \sigma^2)$ denote Gaussian distribution with mean μ and variance σ^2. For a positive integer M, let $[M]$ denote the set $\{1, \dots, M\}$. Let $\sum_{m \neq i}$ denote the summation over all $m \in [M]$ except for $m = i$. Suppose that there are M clients.

From the server's perspective, it is postulated that data $z_1, \dots, z_M$ are generated from the following two-layer Bayesian hierarchical model:

$$\theta_m \mid \theta_0 \overset{\text{IID}}{\sim} \mathcal{N}(\theta_0, \sigma_0^2),\; z_m \mid \theta_m \overset{\text{IID}}{\sim} \mathcal{N}(\theta_m, \sigma_m^2),$$

for all clients with $m = 1, \dots, M$. Here, σ_0^2 is a constant, and $\theta_0 \sim \pi_0(\cdot)$ is a hyperparameter with a non-informative flat prior. The above model represents both the connections and heterogeneity across clients. In particular, each client's data are distributed according to a client-specific parameter (θ_m), which follows a distribution decided by a parent parameter (θ_0). The parent parameter is interpreted as the root of shared information. Without loss of generality, we study client 1's local model as parameterized by θ_1. Under the above model assumption, the parent parameter θ_0 that represents the global model has a posterior distribution $p(\theta_0 \mid z_{1:M}) \sim \mathcal{N}(\theta^{(G)}, v^{(G)})$, where:

$$\theta^{(\text{G})} \triangleq \frac{\sum_{m\in[M]}(\sigma_0^2+\sigma_m^2)^{-1}\theta_m^{(\text{L})}}{\sum_{m\in[M]}(\sigma_0^2+\sigma_m^2)^{-1}}, \quad (1)$$

$$v^{(\text{G})} \triangleq \frac{1}{\sum_{m\in[M]}(\sigma_0^2+\sigma_m^2)^{-1}}.$$

From the perspective of client m, we suppose that the postulated model is the same as above for $m = 2, \dots, M$, and $\theta_1 = \theta_0$. It can be verified that the posterior distributions of θ_1 without and with global Bayesian learning are $p(\theta_1 \mid z_1) \sim \mathcal{N}(\theta_1^{(\text{L})}, v_1^{(\text{L})})$ and $p(\theta_1 \mid z_{1:M}) \sim \mathcal{N}(\theta_1^{(\text{FL})}, v_1^{(\text{FL})})$, respectively, which can be computed as:

$$\theta_1^{(\text{L})} \triangleq z_1, \quad v_1^{(\text{L})} \triangleq \sigma_1^2,$$

$$\theta_1^{(\text{FL})} \triangleq \frac{\sigma_1^{-2}\theta_1^{(\text{L})} + \sum_{m\neq 1}(\sigma_0^2+\sigma_m^2)^{-1}\theta_m^{(\text{L})}}{\sigma_1^{-2} + \sum_{m\neq 1}(\sigma_0^2+\sigma_m^2)^{-1}}, \quad (2)$$

$$v_1^{(\text{FL})} \triangleq \frac{1}{\sigma_1^{-2} + \sum_{m\neq 1}(\sigma_0^2+\sigma_m^2)^{-1}}.$$

The first distribution above describes the learned result of client 1 from its local data, while the second one represents the knowledge from all the clients' data in hindsight. Using the mean square error as risk, the Bayes estimate of θ_1 or θ_0 is the mean of the posterior distribution, namely $\theta_1^{(\text{L})}$ and $\theta_1^{(\text{FL})}$.

The flat prior on θ_0 can be replaced with any other distribution to bake prior knowledge into the calculation. We consider the flat prior because the knowledge of the shared model is often vague in practice. The above posterior mean $\theta_1^{(\text{FL})}$ can be regarded as the optimal point estimation of θ_1 given all the clients' data, thus is referred to as "FL-optimal". $\theta^{(\text{G})}$ can be regarded as the "global-optimal." The posterior variance quantifies the reduced uncertainty conditional on other clients' data. Specifically, we define the following *Personalized FL gain* for client 1 as:

$$\text{GAIN}_1 \triangleq \frac{v_1^{(\text{L})}}{v_1^{(\text{FL})}} = 1 + \sigma_1^2 \sum_{m\neq 1}(\sigma_0^2+\sigma_m^2)^{-1}.$$

Remark 1 (Posterior quantity interpretations) *Each client, say client 1, aims to learn θ_1 in the personalized FL context. Its learned information regarding θ_1 is represented by the Bayesian posterior of θ_1 conditional on either its local data z_1 (without communications with others), or the data $z_{1:M}$ in hindsight (with communications). For the former case, the posterior uncertainty described by $v_1^{(\text{L})}$ depends only on the local data quality σ_1^2. For the latter case, the posterior mean $\theta_1^{(\text{FL})}$ is a weighted sum of clients' local posterior means, and the uncertainty will be reduced by a factor of* GAIN_1*. Since a point estimation of θ_1 is of particular interest in practical implementations, we treat $\theta_1^{(\text{FL})}$ as the theoretical limit in the FL context (recall question Q1).*

Remark 2 (Local training steps to achieve $\theta_1^{(\text{FL})}$) *Suppose that client 1 performs ℓ training steps using its local data and negative log-likelihood loss. We show that with a suitable number of steps and initial value, client 1 can obtain the intended $\theta_1^{(\text{FL})}$. The local objective is:*

$$\theta \mapsto (\theta - z_1)^2/(2\sigma_1^2) = (\theta - \theta_1^{(\text{L})})^2/(2\sigma_1^2), \quad (3)$$

which coincides with the quadratic loss. Let $\eta \in (0, 1)$ denote the learning rate. By running the gradient descent:

$$\theta_1^{\ell} \leftarrow \theta_1^{\ell-1} - \eta\frac{\partial}{\partial\theta}\left((\theta - \theta_1^{(\text{L})})^2/(2\sigma_1^2)\right)\Big|_{\theta_1^{\ell-1}}$$
$$= \theta_1^{\ell-1} - \eta(\theta_1^{\ell-1} - \theta_1^{(\text{L})})/\sigma_1^2 \quad (4)$$

for ℓ steps with initial value θ_1^{INIT}, client 1 obtains:

$$\theta_1^\ell = (1-(1-\sigma_1^{-2}\eta)^\ell)\theta_1^{(\text{L})} + (1-\sigma_1^{-2}\eta)^\ell\theta_1^{\text{INIT}}. \quad (5)$$

It can be verified that Eqn. (5) becomes $\theta_1^{(\text{FL})}$ in Eqn. (2) if and only if:

$$\theta_1^{\text{INIT}} = \frac{\sum_{m\neq 1}(\sigma_0^2+\sigma_m^2)^{-1}\theta_m^{(\text{L})}}{\sum_{m\neq 1}(\sigma_0^2+\sigma_m^2)^{-1}}, \quad (6)$$

$$(1-\sigma_1^{-2}\eta)^\ell = \frac{\sum_{m\neq 1}(\sigma_0^2+\sigma_m^2)^{-1}}{\sigma_1^{-2}+\sum_{m\neq 1}(\sigma_0^2+\sigma_m^2)^{-1}}. \quad (7)$$

In other words, with a suitably chosen initial value θ_1^{INIT}, learning rate η, and the number of (early-stop) steps ℓ, client 1 can obtain the desired $\theta_1^{(\text{FL})}$.

3 Proposed Solution for Personalized FL

Our proposed ActPerFL framework has three key components as detailed in this section: (i) proper initialization for local clients at each round, (ii) automatic determination of the local training steps, (iii) discrepancy-aware aggregation rule for the global model. These components are interconnected and contribute together to ActPerFL's effectiveness. Note that points (i) and (iii) direct ActPerFL to the regions that benefit personalization in the optimization space during local training, which is not considered in prior works such as DITTO (Li et al., 2021) and pFedMe (Dinh et al., 2020b). Therefore, ActPerFL is more than imposing implicit regularization via early stopping.

In this section, we show how the posterior quantities of interest in Section 2 can be connected with FL. Recall that each client m can obtain the FL-optimal solution $\theta_m^{(\text{FL})}$ with the initial value θ_m^{INIT} in Eqn. (6) and tuning parameters η, ℓ in Eqn. (7). Also, it can be shown that θ_m^{INIT} is connected with the global-optimal $\theta^{(\text{G})}$ in Eqn. (1) through

$$\theta_m^{\text{INIT}} = \theta^{(\text{G})} - \frac{(\sigma_0^2+\sigma_m^2)^{-1}}{\sum_{k:\, k\neq m}(\sigma_0^2+\sigma_k^2)^{-1}}(\theta_m^{(\text{L})} - \theta^{(\text{G})}). \quad (8)$$

The initial value θ_m^{INIT} in Eqn. (8) is unknown during training since $\theta_m^{(\text{L})}, \theta^{(\text{G})}$ are both unknown. A natural solution is to update θ_m^{INIT}, $\theta_m^{(\text{L})}$, and $\theta^{(\text{G})}$ iteratively, leading to the following personalized FL rule of our ActPerFL framework.

Generic ActPerFL. At the t-th ($t \geq 1$) round:

- *Client* m receives the latest global model θ^{t-1} from the server (initialized as θ^0), and calculates:

$$\theta_m^{t,\text{INIT}} \triangleq \theta^{t-1} - \frac{(\sigma_0^2+\sigma_m^2)^{-1}(\theta_m^{t-1}-\theta^{t-1})}{\sum_{k:\, k\neq m}(\sigma_0^2+\sigma_k^2)^{-1}}, \quad (9)$$

where θ_m^{t-1} is client m's latest personal parameter at round $t-1$, initialized to be θ^0. Starting from the above $\theta_m^{t,\text{INIT}}$, client m performs gradient descent-based local updates with optimization parameters following Eqn. (7) or its approximations, and obtains a personal parameter θ_m^t.

- *Server* collects θ_m^t and calculates:

$$\theta^t \triangleq \frac{\sum_{m\in[M]}(\sigma_0^2+\sigma_m^2)^{-1}\theta_m^t}{\sum_{m\in[M]}(\sigma_0^2+\sigma_m^2)^{-1}}. \quad (10)$$

In general, the above σ_0^2, σ_m^2 represent "inter-client uncertainty" and "intra-client uncertainty," respectively. When σ_0^2 and σ_m^2's are unknown, they can be approximated asymptotically or using practical finite-sample approximations.

SGD-based practical algorithm for DL. For the above training method, the quantities σ_0^2 and σ_m^2 are crucial as they affect the choice of learning rate η_m and the early-stop rule. However, these two values are unknown in complex learning models. To approximate the uncertainty quantities, we generally treat σ_m^2 as "uncertainty of the local optimal solution $\theta_m^{(\text{L})}$ of client m", and σ_0^2 as "uncertainty of clients' underlying parameters." Assume that for each client m, we had u independent samples of its data and the corresponding local optimal parameter $\theta_{m,1}, \dots, \theta_{m,u}$. We could then estimate σ_m^2 by their *sample variance*. In particular, at round t, we approximate σ_m^2 with:

$$\widehat{\sigma_m^2} = \text{empirical variance of } \{\theta_m^1, \dots, \theta_m^t\}. \quad (11)$$

Likewise, at round t, we estimate σ_0^2 by:

$$\widehat{\sigma_0^2} = \text{empirical variance of } \{\theta_1^t, \dots, \theta_M^t\}. \quad (12)$$

For multi-dimensional parameters, we introduce the following counterpart uncertainty measures. For vectors $x_1, \dots, x_M$, their empirical variance is defined as the trace of $\sum_{m\in[M]}(x_m-\bar{x})(x_m-\bar{x})^{\text{T}}$, which is the sum of entry-wise empirical variances. $\widehat{\sigma_m^2}$ and $\widehat{\sigma_0^2}$ are defined from such empirical variances similar to Eqn. (11) and (12). The above quantities can be calculated recursively online with constant memory (Han et al., 2017). Alg. 1 outlines the workflow of ActPerFL.

4 Experimental Studies

Experimental setup. We evaluate ActPerFL's performance on two NLP datasets: Sentiment140 (Go et al., 2009) and private Amazon Alexa audio data. Sent140 is a text sentiment analysis dataset with two output classes and 772 clients. We generate non-i.i.d. data following FedProx (Li, 2020). The audio dataset is collected for wake-word detection task (i.e., binary classification). This dataset contains 39 thousand hours of training data and 14 thousand hours of test data. We use a two-layer

Algorithm 1 Active Personal FL (ActPerFL)

Input: A server and M clients. Communication rounds T, client activity rate C, client m's local data D_m and learning rate η_m.

for each communication round $t = 1, \ldots T$ **do**
  Sample clients: $\mathbb{M}_t \leftarrow \max(\lfloor C \cdot M \rfloor, 1)$
  for each client $m \in \mathbb{M}_t$ **in parallel do**
    Distribute server model θ^{t-1} to client m
    Estimate $\widehat{\sigma_m^2}$ using Eqn. (11)
    Compute local step l_m from Eqn. (7) and local initialization θ_m^{INIT} via Eqn. (6)
    $\theta_m^t \leftarrow LocalTrain(\theta_m^{\mathrm{INIT}}, \eta_m, l_m; D_m)$
  Server estimates $\widehat{\sigma_0^2}$ using Eqn. (12)
  Server updates global model θ^t via Eqn. (10)

LSTM model and an 11-layer CNN model for these two datasets, respectively. For comparison, we also evaluate the personalization performance of FedAvg (McMahan et al., 2017), DITTO (Li et al., 2021), PerFedAvg (Fallah et al., 2020b), and pFedMe (Dinh et al., 2020b).

4.1 Results on Alexa Audio Data

For Alexa audio data, we use a CNN that is pre-trained on the training data of different device types (i.e., heterogeneous data) as the initial global model to *warm-start* FL training. The personalization task aims to improve the wake-word detection performance at the *device type level*. We assume there are five clients in the FL system and all of them participate in each round. Each client has the training data for a specific device type.

Evaluation metric. We evaluate the performance using the pre-trained model (for warm-start) as the *baseline*. To compare different FL algorithms, we use the *relative false accept (FA)* value of the resulting model when the associated relative false reject (FR) is close to one as the metric. So a smaller relative FA is preferred. Here, the relative FA and FR are computed using the baseline.

For comparison, we implement FedAvg and DITTO with both equal-weighted and sample size-based model averaging (denoted by the suffix '-e' and '-w', respectively) during aggregation. For PerFedAvg (Fallah et al., 2020b), we use its first-order approximation and the equal-weighted aggregation. We did not report pFedMe (Dinh et al., 2020b) due to its divergence with various hyper-parameters. Table 1 summarizes the performance of the updated global model. The results show that ActPerFL achieves the lowest relative FA, thus obtaining the best global model. We further compare the personalization performance of local models obtained by different FL algorithms in Table 2.

Table 1: Detection performance (relative FA) of the *global model* on the test dataset.

FL methods	Device Types				
	A	B	C	D	E
ActPerFL	**0.92**	**0.94**	**0.91**	**0.91**	1.01
FedAvg-w	8.39	4.00	12.80	8.61	10.62
FedAvg-e	0.97	0.96	1.00	0.92	1.00
DITTO-w	8.38	4.00	12.75	8.61	10.23
DITTO-e	0.97	0.95	1.00	0.93	**0.99**
PerFedAvg	1.06	0.98	1.08	0.93	1.01

Table 2: Detection performance (relative FA) of the *personalized models* on a test dataset.

FL methods	Device Type				
	A	B	C	D	E
ActPerFL	**0.93**	**0.91**	**0.90**	**0.90**	0.99
FedAvg-e	0.95	0.95	0.93	0.91	0.98
DITTO-e	0.97	0.96	0.93	0.91	0.96
PerFedAvg	1.02	1.11	1.08	1.00	**0.93**

4.2 Results on Sent140 Text Data

In this experiment, we also use warm-start by training a global model from scratch with FedAvg for 200 rounds for initializing other FL algorithms. Then, we continue FL training with various FL methods for another 400 rounds. Figure 1 compares the training and test accuracy of the personalized models obtained by different FL algorithms where the accuracy is aggregated across clients. We can see that both ActPerFL and FedAvg demonstrate better convergence performance compared to DITTO (Li et al., 2021), pFedMe (Dinh et al., 2020b), and PerFedAvg (Fallah et al., 2020b).

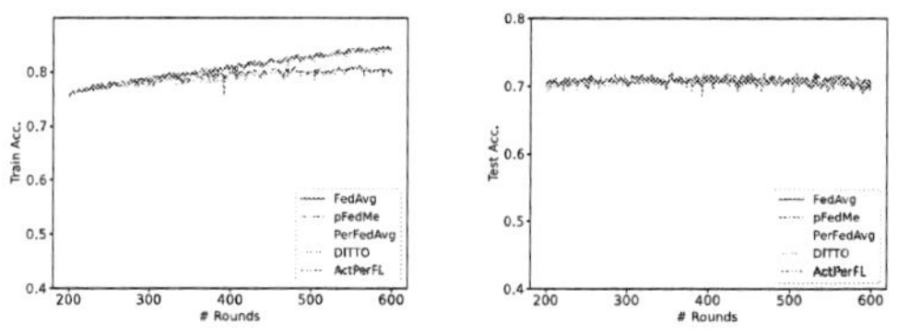

(a) Training accuracy. (b) Test accuracy.

Figure 1: Performance of FL methods on Sent140 data.

5 Concluding Remarks

We proposed ActPerFL to address the challenge of balancing local model training and global model aggregation in personalized FL. Our solution adaptively adjusts local training with automated hyper-parameter selection and performs uncertainty-weighted global aggregation. Empirical studies show that ActPerFL can achieve promising performance on NLP applications.

References

Enmao Diao, Jie Ding, and Vahid Tarokh. 2020. HeteroFL: Computation and communication efficient federated learning for heterogeneous clients. In *International Conference on Learning Representations*.

Enmao Diao, Jie Ding, and Vahid Tarokh. 2021. SemiFL: Communication efficient semi-supervised federated learning with unlabeled clients. *arXiv preprint arXiv:2106.01432*.

Canh T Dinh, Nguyen H Tran, and Tuan Dung Nguyen. 2020a. Personalized federated learning with moreau envelopes. *arXiv preprint arXiv:2006.08848*.

Canh T Dinh, Nguyen H Tran, and Tuan Dung Nguyen. 2020b. Personalized federated learning with moreau envelopes. *arXiv preprint arXiv:2006.08848*.

Alireza Fallah, Aryan Mokhtari, and Asuman Ozdaglar. 2020a. Personalized federated learning: A meta-learning approach. *arXiv preprint arXiv:2002.07948*.

Alireza Fallah, Aryan Mokhtari, and Asuman Ozdaglar. 2020b. Personalized federated learning: A meta-learning approach. *arXiv preprint arXiv:2002.07948*.

Alec Go, Richa Bhayani, and Lei Huang. 2009. Twitter sentiment classification using distant supervision. *CS224N project report, Stanford*, 1(12):2009.

Qiuyi Han, Jie Ding, Edoardo M Airoldi, and Vahid Tarokh. 2017. Slants: Sequential adaptive nonlinear modeling of time series. *IEEE Transactions on Signal Processing*, 65(19):4994–5005.

Jakub Konevcny, H Brendan McMahan, Felix X Yu, Peter Richtárik, Ananda Theertha Suresh, and Dave Bacon. 2016. Federated learning: Strategies for improving communication efficiency. *arXiv preprint arXiv:1610.05492*.

Tian Li. 2020. Github repo of paper federated optimization in heterogeneous networks. `https://github.com/litian96/FedProx`.

Tian Li, Shengyuan Hu, Ahmad Beirami, and Virginia Smith. 2021. Ditto: Fair and robust federated learning through personalization. In *International Conference on Machine Learning*, pages 6357–6368. PMLR.

Wei Yang Bryan Lim, Nguyen Cong Luong, Dinh Thai Hoang, Yutao Jiao, Ying-Chang Liang, Qiang Yang, Dusit Niyato, and Chunyan Miao. 2020. Federated learning in mobile edge networks: A comprehensive survey. *IEEE Communications Surveys & Tutorials*.

Brendan McMahan, Eider Moore, Daniel Ramage, Seth Hampson, and Blaise Aguera y Arcas. 2017. Communication-efficient learning of deep networks from decentralized data. In *Proc. AISTATS*, pages 1273–1282. PMLR.

Amanda Purington, Jessie G Taft, Shruti Sannon, Natalya N Bazarova, and Samuel Hardman Taylor. 2017. "alexa is my new bff" social roles, user satisfaction, and personification of the amazon echo. In *Proceedings of the 2017 CHI conference extended abstracts on human factors in computing systems*, pages 2853–2859.

Scaling Language Model Size in Cross-Device Federated Learning

Jae Hun Ro* and **Theresa Breiner** and **Lara McConnaughey**
Mingqing Chen and **Ananda Theertha Suresh** and **Shankar Kumar** and **Rajiv Mathews**

Google

*jaero@google.com

Abstract

Most studies in cross-device federated learning focus on small models, due to the server-client communication and on-device computation bottlenecks. In this work, we leverage various techniques for mitigating these bottlenecks to train larger language models in cross-device federated learning. With systematic applications of partial model training, quantization, efficient transfer learning, and communication-efficient optimizers, we are able to train a 21M parameter Transformer that achieves the same perplexity as that of a similarly sized LSTM with $\sim 10\times$ smaller client-to-server communication cost and 11% lower perplexity than smaller LSTMs commonly studied in literature.

1 Introduction

Federated learning is a distributed training technique, where a model is trained on data distributed across clients or edge devices without user-generated data ever leaving the device, providing an additional layer of privacy and security (Konečný et al., 2016b,a; McMahan et al., 2017). We refer readers to (Li et al., 2020; Kairouz et al., 2021) for a detailed literature survey on federated learning. Federated learning has been used in several applications including virtual keyboard applications (Hard et al., 2018), keyword spotting (Hard et al., 2020), and healthcare (Brisimi et al., 2018).

Language models (LM) have many uses in language-based applications including virtual keyboard (Chen et al., 2019; Zhang et al., 2021) and automatic speech recognition (Kannan et al., 2018; Variani et al., 2020; Gruenstein et al., 2021). Recently, there has been increased interest in training progressively larger and deeper LMs with impressive quality improvements in downstream tasks, including question answering, text classification, and text summarization (Devlin et al., 2019; Dai et al., 2019; Yang et al., 2019; Irie et al., 2019; Kaplan et al., 2020). These models tend to be variants of the Transformer (Vaswani et al., 2017).

Federated learning is typically studied in two scenarios: *cross-silo*, where the number of clients is small, and *cross-device*, where the number of clients can be in the order of millions (Hard et al., 2018). In this work we focus on cross-device, where devices are typically edge devices such as cell phones, with limited computation and communication capabilities. Hence, the major benchmark LMs tend to be very limited in size (McMahan et al., 2017, 2018; Caldas et al., 2019a; Reddi et al., 2020; Sim et al., 2021) because memory, computation, and communication are critical bottlenecks (Kairouz et al., 2021). In particular, previous works that train federated LMs in production settings have used coupled input forget gate (CIFG) long short-term memory (LSTM) models with fewer than 4 million parameters (Hard et al., 2018; Chen et al., 2019; Ramaswamy et al., 2020). These resource constraints have motivated research into various efficient algorithms for training larger models with federated learning (Konečný et al., 2016b; Hamer et al., 2020). However, most of these techniques are still evaluated on relatively small models compared to their server-based counterparts. In this work, we systematically evaluate multiple strategies for mitigating communication and computation costs of training larger LMs to determine if the impressive quality gains from larger models can also be achieved in cross-device federated learning.

While there are previous works on *efficient* Transformers (Tay et al., 2020, 2021), we forgo these efficient variants as they may actually be more inefficient when sequences are short (Katharopoulos et al., 2020; Choromanski et al., 2021). Additionally, Lin et al. (2020); Liu and Miller (2020); Hilmkil et al. (2021) trained large Transformer models in the cross-silo setting, where devices have more resources, whereas we focus on the resource-constrained cross-device setting.

Proceedings of the First Workshop on Federated Learning for Natural Language Processing (FL4NLP 2022), pages 6 - 20

Recent large LMs, such as GPT-3 (Brown et al., 2020), contain hundreds of billions of parameters, which is substantially bigger than the memory limits of edge devices. Therefore in this work, we consider *large* models to be at most 25 million parameters, which is still considerably larger than existing models trained on-device.

The rest of the paper is organized as follows. In Section 2, we overview our contributions. In Section 3, we detail the dataset and models. We then analyze techniques to reduce the per-round cost in Section 4, and the number of communication rounds in Section 5. Finally in Section 6, we combine techniques and demonstrate that large Transformers can be trained using many fewer rounds and significantly lower communication and computation cost.

2 Our contributions

We explore two regimes: small models typically studied in cross-device federated learning with fewer than 5M parameters and new larger models with at most 25M parameters. We study two architectures: CIFG-LSTM (Hochreiter and Schmidhuber, 1997), or LSTM for simplicity, (Hard et al., 2018) and Transformer (Vaswani et al., 2017). Our contributions are the following:

- We are the first to investigate Transformer LMs with 25M parameters for cross-device federated learning, which we find outperform LSTMs of similar size.
- We demonstrate that large models substantially outperform small models on standard tasks but at much higher communication and computation costs, requiring $4\times$ the communication cost per round.
- We investigate quantization and partial model training to address the per round communication and computation cost. With quantization, we achieve similar perplexity with half the download cost and one quarter of the upload cost, reducing total communication cost by 62.5%. Partial model training can further reduce the upload cost by 60%.
- We study transfer learning as a method of reducing the number of communication rounds and show that centralized pretraining on a suitable alternate corpus reduces the total communication rounds by $3\times$.
- We show that the combination of above techniques can be used to train a Large Transformer with the same perplexity as that of a similarly sized LSTM with $\sim 10\times$ the smaller client-to-server communication cost.

3 Dataset and models

In this section, we describe the models and dataset used in the rest of the paper. We train on the Stack Overflow federated dataset from TFF (2018), which contains posts from the public forum grouped by username. Following trends in training Transformers, we use sentence-piece (Kudo and Richardson, 2018) for sub-word tokenization with a vocabulary size of 4K. The sentence-piece model is computed based on the entire Stack Overflow training corpus in an offline process on server. During federated learning, this fixed sentence-piece model is transmitted to each client to encode the local text data. Doing so provides greater coverage for cross-dataset applications as well as potential downstream speech applications such as ASR (Li et al., 2021; Sim et al., 2021). We measure performance on next-subword prediction using test perplexity. See Appendix A for descriptive dataset statistics. All experiments were implemented using JAX (Bradbury et al., 2018) and FedJAX (Ro et al., 2021) federated simulation libraries.

We first did a hyperparameter search for each model and size ($\leq$ 5M and $\leq$ 25M), with FedAdam (Reddi et al., 2020), or FedAvg for simplicity, with 200 clients per round for 3K rounds, resulting in four models: *Small LSTM* (4.7M), *Large LSTM* (18.8M), *Small Transformer* (4.1M), and *Large Transformer* (21M).

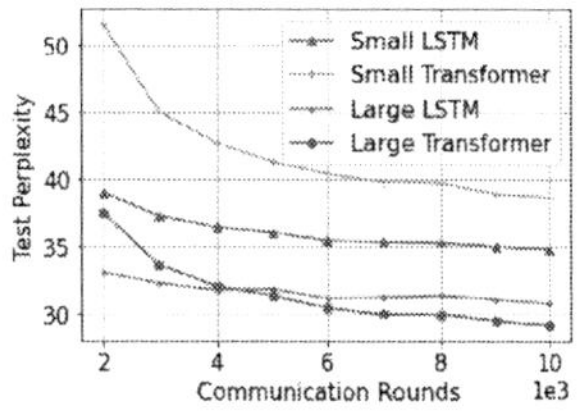

Figure 1: Test perplexity over communication rounds for each class and size of model.

We then trained the chosen architectures with 800 clients per round for 10K rounds in Figure 1. As expected, the larger variants significantly outperform their smaller counterparts with the Large Transformer achieving the best perplexity. However, the larger models are more expensive to train per round and although the Large Transformer achieves the best perplexity, it only surpasses the Large LSTM after 4K rounds. Next, we focus on techniques to reduce this cost per round and number of rounds. For more details about the architecture search, the selected models, and their performance, see Appendix A.

4 Cost per round

The larger models have 18.8M and 21M parameters (150MB and 168MB, at 32 bits per parameter) which need to be downloaded, trained, and uploaded at each round, a strain on both communication and computation on device. There are often strict time or transfer byte limits for each round of training, which can prohibit some devices from training these models due to slower transfer/processing speeds (Kairouz et al., 2021). We show that we can significantly reduce these costs by partial model training and quantization techniques.

Partial model training: Training only a subset of the model can reduce the computational cost of training and has been examined in both federated (Caldas et al., 2019b; Yang et al., 2021) and non-federated (Kovaleva et al., 2019) settings. Additionally, reducing the number of trainable parameters can also decrease communication cost since only the trainable parameters need to be uploaded.

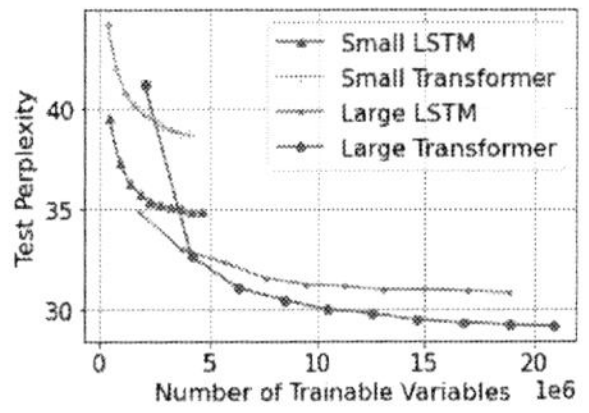

Figure 2: Test perplexity as a function of number of trainable variables.

We follow the Partial Variable Training (PVT) per client per round strategy (Yang et al., 2021) as it only freezes a subset of the original model and can be applied generally to multiple model architecture types. For more experiment details, see Appendix B. We report test perplexity as a function of number of trainable variables in Figure 2. Large LSTM seems to be able to handle more aggressive parameter freezing compared to Large Transformer in terms of quality regression. However, training only 40% of variables for the Large Transformer (6.3M) achieves better performance than the full Large LSTM (18.8M).

Quantization: To reduce communication costs, various quantization strategies can decrease the number of bits required to represent model parameters (Bernstein et al., 2018; Reisizadeh et al., 2020; Gandikota et al., 2021; Vargaftik et al., 2021). We examine stochastic k-level uniform quantization (Alistarh et al., 2017; Suresh et al., 2017) as it can be applied to model parameters on download (server-to-client) and model updates on upload (client-to-server) communication with adjustable levels of compression, and compare with TernGrad, an upload technique (Wen et al., 2017).

We focus analysis on larger models which are more affected by quantization. The LSTM appears more "quantizable" during download than the Transformer, with less regression in Figure 3. The perplexity of the Transformer with 16 download bits matches that of the baseline Transformer and with 12 bits its perplexity is close to that of the LSTM.

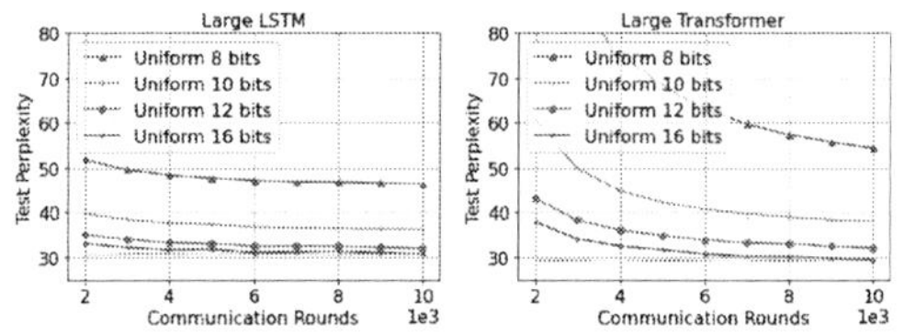

Figure 3: Test perplexity over communication rounds for varying download quantization levels, with upload quantization fixed to 8 bits. Dashed line shows the baseline without quantization.

For both the models, 8 bit upload matches the corresponding baselines, or even 6 bits for the LSTM in Figure 4. TernGrad, requiring $\log_2(3)$ bits, outperforms the 4 bit in the Transformer but not for the LSTM in Figure 5. More details are in Appendix C.

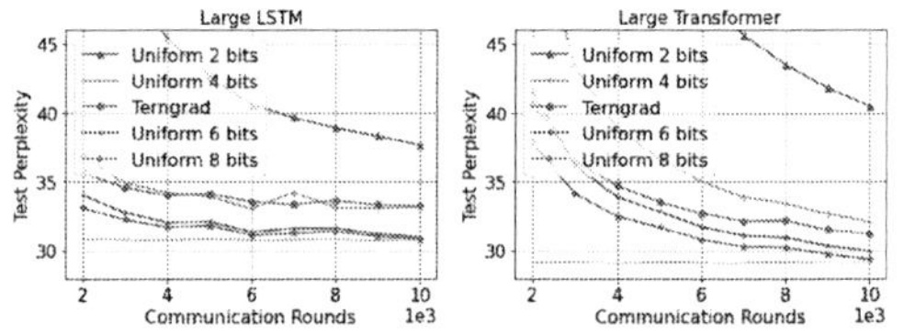

Figure 4: Test perplexity over communication rounds for varying upload quantization levels, with download quantization fixed to 16 bits. TernGrad is comparable to uniform with about 1.6 bits. Dashed line shows the baseline without quantization.

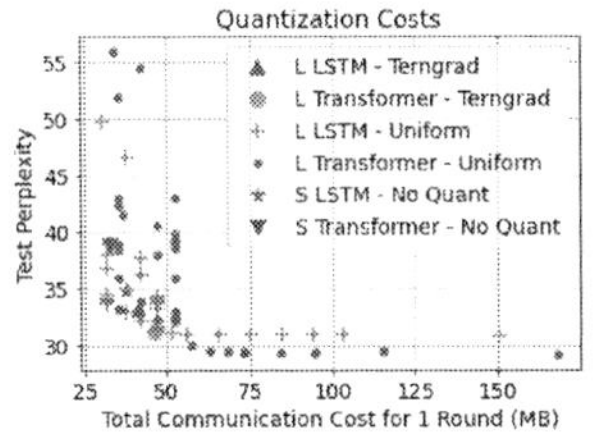

Figure 5: Test set perplexity versus total communication cost (download + upload) in a single round of training, for each quantization algorithm. Uniform settings include points for varying quantization bits.

5 Number of communication rounds

Transfer learning: Transfer learning leverages pretrained models to improve model quality (Houlsby et al., 2019). By pretraining, the number of communication rounds required for model convergence can be significantly reduced (Stremmel and Singh, 2020).

We use two datasets for pretraining: a large corpus of digitized books (Zhang et al., 2021) and the One Billion Word Benchmark (LM1B) (Chelba et al., 2014). After pretraining using synchronous SGD for 30M steps, we finetune on Stack Overflow using FedAvg. For additional details, see Appendix D. We report results for each of the pretraining datasets and random initialization in Figure 6.

Books consistently outperforms LM1B for both the LSTM and Transformer. Pretraining greatly benefits the Large Transformer compared to the Large LSTM, reducing the number of rounds needed to reach the final 10K without pretraining by 4K rounds. Furthermore, at round 2K, the Large Transformer already outperforms the Large LSTM, making the number of rounds needed for training similar to that of smaller models used in mobile keyboard prediction (Hard et al., 2018).

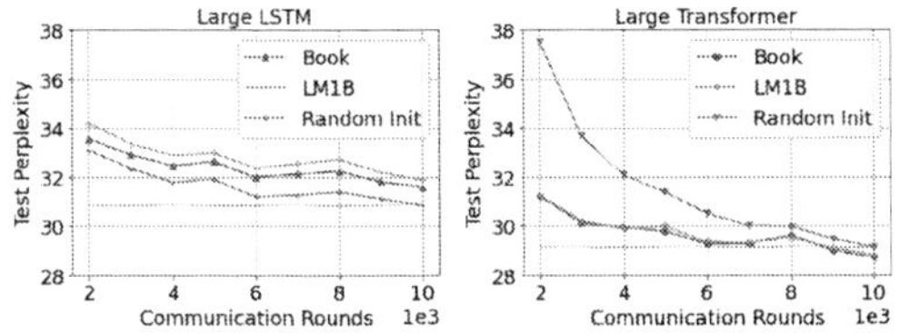

Figure 6: Test perplexity over communication comparing pretraining corpora. Dashed line is the final perplexity reached by the randomly initialized model.

Different optimizers: Since the introduction of FedAvg, several variations continue to be developed (Li et al., 2018; Hamer et al., 2020; Reddi

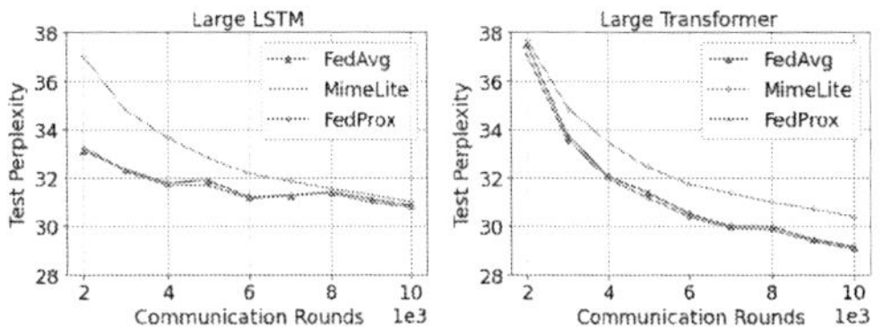

Figure 7: Test perplexity over communication rounds for each model and algorithm.

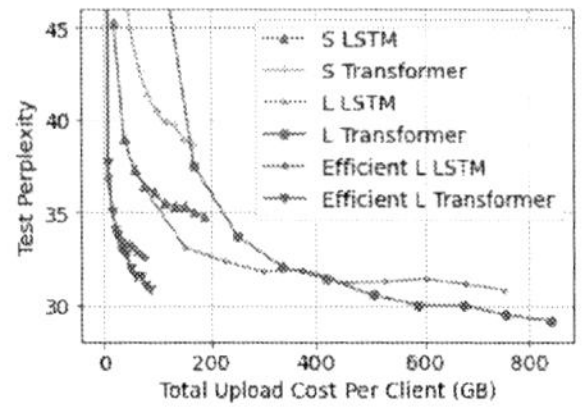

Figure 8: Test perplexity over total uploaded gigabytes per client for each class of model.

et al., 2020). Specifically, we examine MimeLite (Karimireddy et al., 2020) and FedProx (Li et al., 2018) as they have been shown to reduce the total amount of rounds required for provable convergence. However, in Figure 7, FedProx and MimeLite do not improve convergence speed over FedAvg. More details can be found in Appendix E.

6 Combination of techniques

We experiment with combining partial model training, quantization, and transfer learning to train *efficient* larger models. For these experiments, we train on just 40% of trainable parameters with PVT and warm start after pretraining on the Books corpus. Combining download quantization with these techniques did not perform as well, so we only apply 8 bit uniform quantization on upload, which is the tightest communication bottleneck (Statista.com (2021) reports that mobile upload speeds worldwide are over 4× slower than download as of May 2021). For the full experiment details, refer to Appendix F. We report the test perplexity in terms of total upload communication cost in Figure 8. Restricting for small upload costs (< 200GB), the efficient models outperform all others with the efficient Large Transformer yielding the best perplexity. Furthermore, the efficient Large Transformer also achieves the same perplexity as the Large LSTM with no efficient techniques.

7 Conclusion

We systematically studied several techniques for addressing the communication and computation bottlenecks of federated learning. We further demonstrated that these techniques, individually or in combination, can scale to larger models in cross-device federated learning. Extending this study to other architectures and efficient strategies remains an interesting open question.

References

Dan Alistarh, Demjan Grubic, Jerry Li, Ryota Tomioka, and Milan Vojnovic. 2017. Qsgd: Communication-efficient sgd via gradient quantization and encoding. *Advances in Neural Information Processing Systems*, 30.

Jeremy Bernstein, Yu-Xiang Wang, Kamyar Azizzadenesheli, and Animashree Anandkumar. 2018. signsgd: Compressed optimisation for non-convex problems. In *International Conference on Machine Learning*, pages 560–569. PMLR.

James Bradbury, Roy Frostig, Peter Hawkins, Matthew James Johnson, Chris Leary, Dougal Maclaurin, George Necula, Adam Paszke, Jake VanderPlas, Skye Wanderman-Milne, and Qiao Zhang. 2018. JAX: composable transformations of Python+NumPy programs.

Theodora S Brisimi, Ruidi Chen, Theofanie Mela, Alex Olshevsky, Ioannis Ch Paschalidis, and Wei Shi. 2018. Federated learning of predictive models from federated electronic health records. *International journal of medical informatics*, 112:59–67.

Tom B. Brown, Benjamin Mann, Nick Ryder, Melanie Subbiah, Jared Kaplan, Prafulla Dhariwal, Arvind Neelakantan, Pranav Shyam, Girish Sastry, Amanda Askell, Sandhini Agarwal, Ariel Herbert-Voss, Gretchen Krueger, Tom Henighan, Rewon Child, Aditya Ramesh, Daniel M. Ziegler, Jeffrey Wu, Clemens Winter, Christopher Hesse, Mark Chen, Eric Sigler, Mateusz Litwin, Scott Gray, Benjamin Chess, Jack Clark, Christopher Berner, Sam McCandlish, Alec Radford, Ilya Sutskever, and Dario Amodei. 2020. Language models are few-shot learners.

Sebastian Caldas, Sai Meher Karthik Duddu, Peter Wu, Tian Li, Jakub Konečný, H. Brendan McMahan, Virginia Smith, and Ameet Talwalkar. 2019a. Leaf: A benchmark for federated settings.

Sebastian Caldas, Jakub Konečny, H. Brendan McMahan, and Ameet Talwalkar. 2019b. Expanding the reach of federated learning by reducing client resource requirements.

Ciprian Chelba, Tomas Mikolov, Mike Schuster, Qi Ge, T. Brants, Phillip Todd Koehn, and Tony Robinson. 2014. One billion word benchmark for measuring progress in statistical language modeling. *ArXiv*, abs/1312.3005.

Mingqing Chen, Ananda Theertha Suresh, Rajiv Mathews, Adeline Wong, Cyril Allauzen, Françoise Beaufays, and Michael Riley. 2019. Federated learning of n-gram language models. In *Proceedings of the 23rd Conference on Computational Natural Language Learning (CoNLL)*, pages 121–130, Hong Kong, China. Association for Computational Linguistics.

Krzysztof Marcin Choromanski, Valerii Likhosherstov, David Dohan, Xingyou Song, Andreea Gane, Tamas Sarlos, Peter Hawkins, Jared Quincy Davis, Afroz Mohiuddin, Lukasz Kaiser, David Benjamin Belanger, Lucy J Colwell, and Adrian Weller. 2021. Rethinking attention with performers. In *International Conference on Learning Representations*.

Zihang Dai, Zhilin Yang, Yiming Yang, Jaime Carbonell, Quoc Le, and Ruslan Salakhutdinov. 2019. Transformer-XL: Attentive language models beyond a fixed-length context. In *Proceedings of the 57th Annual Meeting of the Association for Computational Linguistics*, pages 2978–2988, Florence, Italy. Association for Computational Linguistics.

Jacob Devlin, Ming-Wei Chang, Kenton Lee, and Kristina Toutanova. 2019. BERT: Pre-training of deep bidirectional transformers for language understanding. In *Proceedings of the 2019 Conference of the North American Chapter of the Association for Computational Linguistics: Human Language Technologies, Volume 1 (Long and Short Papers)*, pages 4171–4186, Minneapolis, Minnesota. Association for Computational Linguistics.

John Duchi, Elad Hazan, and Yoram Singer. 2011. Adaptive subgradient methods for online learning and stochastic optimization. *Journal of Machine Learning Research*, 12(61):2121–2159.

Venkata Gandikota, Daniel Kane, Raj Kumar Maity, and Arya Mazumdar. 2021. vqsgd: Vector quantized stochastic gradient descent. In *International Conference on Artificial Intelligence and Statistics*, pages 2197–2205. PMLR.

Alex Gruenstein, Anmol Gulati, Arun Narayanan, Bo Li, Cal Peyser, Chung-Cheng Chiu, Cyril Allauzen, David Johannes Rybach, Diamantino A. Caseiro, Ehsan Variani, Emmanuel Guzman, Ian Carmichael McGraw, James Qin, Jiahui Yu, Michael D. Riley, Pat Rondon, Qiao Liang, Quoc-Nam Le-The, Rami Botros, Ruoming Pang, Sepand Mavandadi, Shuo yiin Chang, Tara N Sainath, Trevor Deatrick Strohman, W. Ronny Huang, Wei Li, Yanzhang (Ryan) He, Yonghui Wu, and Yu Zhang. 2021. An efficient streaming non-recurrent on-device end-to-end model with improvements to rare-word modeling.

Jenny Hamer, Mehryar Mohri, and Ananda Theertha Suresh. 2020. Fedboost: A communication-efficient algorithm for federated learning. In *International Conference on Machine Learning*, pages 3973–3983. PMLR.

Andrew Hard, Kurt Partridge, Cameron Nguyen, Niranjan Subrahmanya, Aishanee Shah, Pai Zhu, Ignacio Lopez Moreno, and Rajiv Mathews. 2020. Training keyword spotting models on non-iid data with federated learning. In *Interspeech*.

Andrew Hard, Kanishka Rao, Rajiv Mathews, Françoise Beaufays, Sean Augenstein, Hubert Eichner, Chloé Kiddon, and Daniel Ramage. 2018. Federated learning for mobile keyboard prediction. *arXiv preprint arXiv:1811.03604*.

Agrin Hilmkil, Sebastian Callh, Matteo Barbieri, Leon René Sütfeld, Edvin Listo Zec, and Olof Mogren. 2021. Scaling federated learning for fine-tuning of large language models. In *International Conference on Applications of Natural Language to Information Systems*, pages 15–23. Springer.

Sepp Hochreiter and Jürgen Schmidhuber. 1997. Long short-term memory. *Neural computation*, 9(8):1735–1780.

Neil Houlsby, Andrei Giurgiu, Stanislaw Jastrzebski, Bruna Morrone, Quentin De Laroussilhe, Andrea Gesmundo, Mona Attariyan, and Sylvain Gelly. 2019. Parameter-efficient transfer learning for NLP. In *Proceedings of the 36th International Conference on Machine Learning*, volume 97 of *Proceedings of Machine Learning Research*, pages 2790–2799. PMLR.

Kazuki Irie, Albert Zeyer, Ralf Schlüter, and Hermann Ney. 2019. Language modeling with deep transformers. *Interspeech 2019*.

Peter Kairouz et al. 2021. Advances and open problems in federated learning. *Foundations and Trends® in Machine Learning*, 14(1).

Anjuli Kannan, Yonghui Wu, Patrick Nguyen, Tara N. Sainath, ZhiJeng Chen, and Rohit Prabhavalkar. 2018. An analysis of incorporating an external language model into a sequence-to-sequence model. In *2018 IEEE International Conference on Acoustics, Speech and Signal Processing (ICASSP)*, pages 1–5828.

Jared Kaplan, Sam McCandlish, Tom Henighan, Tom B. Brown, Benjamin Chess, Rewon Child, Scott Gray, Alec Radford, Jeffrey Wu, and Dario Amodei. 2020. Scaling laws for neural language models.

Sai Praneeth Karimireddy, Martin Jaggi, Satyen Kale, Mehryar Mohri, Sashank J Reddi, Sebastian U Stich, and Ananda Theertha Suresh. 2020. Mime: Mimicking centralized stochastic algorithms in federated learning. *arXiv preprint arXiv:2008.03606*.

Angelos Katharopoulos, Apoorv Vyas, Nikolaos Pappas, and Francois Fleuret. 2020. Transformers are rnns: Fast autoregressive transformers with linear attention. In *ICML 2020: 37th International Conference on Machine Learning*, volume 1, pages 5156–5165.

Jakub Konečný, H Brendan McMahan, Daniel Ramage, and Peter Richtárik. 2016a. Federated optimization: Distributed machine learning for on-device intelligence. *arXiv preprint arXiv:1610.02527*.

Jakub Konečný, H Brendan McMahan, Felix X Yu, Peter Richtárik, Ananda Theertha Suresh, and Dave Bacon. 2016b. Federated learning: Strategies for improving communication efficiency. *arXiv preprint arXiv:1610.05492*.

Olga Kovaleva, Alexey Romanov, Anna Rogers, and Anna Rumshisky. 2019. Revealing the dark secrets of BERT. In *Proceedings of the 2019 Conference on Empirical Methods in Natural Language Processing and the 9th International Joint Conference on Natural Language Processing (EMNLP-IJCNLP)*, pages 4365–4374, Hong Kong, China. Association for Computational Linguistics.

Taku Kudo and John Richardson. 2018. SentencePiece: A simple and language independent subword tokenizer and detokenizer for neural text processing. In *Proceedings of the 2018 Conference on Empirical Methods in Natural Language Processing: System Demonstrations*, pages 66–71, Brussels, Belgium. Association for Computational Linguistics.

Bo Li, Anmol Gulati, Jiahui Yu, Tara N. Sainath, Chung-Cheng Chiu, Arun Narayanan, Shuo-Yiin Chang, Ruoming Pang, Yanzhang He, James Qin, Wei Han, Qiao Liang, Yu Zhang, Trevor Strohman, and Yonghui Wu. 2021. A better and faster end-to-end model for streaming ASR. In *IEEE International Conference on Acoustics, Speech and Signal Processing, ICASSP 2021, Toronto, ON, Canada, June 6-11, 2021*, pages 5634–5638. IEEE.

Tian Li, Anit Kumar Sahu, Ameet Talwalkar, and Virginia Smith. 2020. Federated learning: Challenges, methods, and future directions. *IEEE Signal Processing Magazine*, 37(3):50–60.

Tian Li, Anit Kumar Sahu, Manzil Zaheer, Maziar Sanjabi, Ameet Talwalkar, and Virginia Smith. 2018. Federated optimization in heterogeneous networks. *arXiv preprint arXiv:1812.06127*.

Tao Lin, Lingjing Kong, Sebastian U Stich, and Martin Jaggi. 2020. Ensemble distillation for robust model fusion in federated learning. *Advances in Neural Information Processing Systems*, 33:2351–2363.

Dianbo Liu and Tim Miller. 2020. Federated pretraining and fine tuning of bert using clinical notes from multiple silos. *arXiv preprint arXiv:2002.08562*.

Brendan McMahan, Eider Moore, Daniel Ramage, Seth Hampson, and Blaise Aguera y Arcas. 2017. Communication-efficient learning of deep networks from decentralized data. In *Artificial Intelligence and Statistics*, pages 1273–1282. PMLR.

H. Brendan McMahan, Daniel Ramage, Kunal Talwar, and Li Zhang. 2018. Learning differentially private recurrent language models.

Swaroop Ramaswamy, Om Thakkar, Rajiv Mathews, Galen Andrew, H. Brendan McMahan, and Françoise Beaufays. 2020. Training production language models without memorizing user data.

Sashank Reddi, Zachary Charles, Manzil Zaheer, Zachary Garrett, Keith Rush, Jakub Konečný, Sanjiv Kumar, and H. Brendan McMahan. 2020. Adaptive federated optimization.

Amirhossein Reisizadeh, Aryan Mokhtari, Hamed Hassani, Ali Jadbabaie, and Ramtin Pedarsani. 2020. Fedpaq: A communication-efficient federated learning method with periodic averaging and quantization. In *Proceedings of the Twenty Third International Conference on Artificial Intelligence and Statistics*, volume 108 of *Proceedings of Machine Learning Research*, pages 2021–2031. PMLR.

Jae Hun Ro, Ananda Theertha Suresh, and Ke Wu. 2021. Fedjax: Federated learning simulation with jax. *arXiv preprint arXiv:2108.02117*.

Khe Chai Sim, Angad Chandorkar, Fan Gao, Mason Chua, Tsendsuren Munkhdalai, and Françoise Beaufays. 2021. Robust Continuous On-Device Personalization for Automatic Speech Recognition. In *Proc. Interspeech 2021*, pages 1284–1288.

Statista.com. 2021. Average mobile and fixed broadband download and upload speeds worldwide as of May 2021. Accessed September 26, 2021.

Joel Stremmel and Arjun Singh. 2020. Pretraining federated text models for next word prediction. *CoRR*, abs/2005.04828.

Ananda Theertha Suresh, Felix X Yu, Sanjiv Kumar, and H Brendan McMahan. 2017. Distributed mean estimation with limited communication. In *Proceedings of the 34th International Conference on Machine Learning-Volume 70*, pages 3329–3337. JMLR. org.

Yi Tay, Mostafa Dehghani, Samira Abnar, Yikang Shen, Dara Bahri, Philip Pham, Jinfeng Rao, Liu Yang, Sebastian Ruder, and Donald Metzler. 2021. Long range arena : A benchmark for efficient transformers. In *International Conference on Learning Representations*.

Yi Tay, Mostafa Dehghani, Dara Bahri, and Donald Metzler. 2020. Efficient transformers: A survey.

TFF. 2018. Tensorflow federated.

Shay Vargaftik, Ran Ben-Basat, Amit Portnoy, Gal Mendelson, Yaniv Ben-Itzhak, and Michael Mitzenmacher. 2021. DRIVE: One-bit distributed mean estimation. In *Advances in Neural Information Processing Systems*.

Ehsan Variani, David Rybach, Cyril Allauzen, and Michael Riley. 2020. Hybrid autoregressive transducer (hat).

Ashish Vaswani, Noam Shazeer, Niki Parmar, Jakob Uszkoreit, Llion Jones, Aidan N Gomez, Ł ukasz Kaiser, and Illia Polosukhin. 2017. Attention is all you need. In *Advances in Neural Information Processing Systems*, volume 30. Curran Associates, Inc.

Wei Wen, Cong Xu, Feng Yan, Chunpeng Wu, Yandan Wang, Yiran Chen, and Hai Li. 2017. Terngrad: Ternary gradients to reduce communication in distributed deep learning. *CoRR*, abs/1705.07878.

Tien-Ju Yang, Dhruv Guliani, Françoise Beaufays, and Giovanni Motta. 2021. Partial variable training for efficient on-device federated learning.

Zhilin Yang, Zihang Dai, Yiming Yang, Jaime Carbonell, Russ R Salakhutdinov, and Quoc V Le. 2019. Xlnet: Generalized autoregressive pretraining for language understanding. In *Advances in Neural Information Processing Systems*, volume 32. Curran Associates, Inc.

Hao Zhang, You-Chi Cheng, Shankar Kumar, Mingqing Chen, and Rajiv Mathews. 2021. Position-invariant truecasing with a word-and-character hierarchical recurrent neural network. *ArXiv*, abs/2108.11943.

Barret Zoph, Golnaz Ghiasi, Tsung-Yi Lin, Yin Cui, Hanxiao Liu, Ekin Dogus Cubuk, and Quoc Le. 2020. Rethinking pre-training and self-training. In *NeurIPS*.

Appendix

A Dataset and models

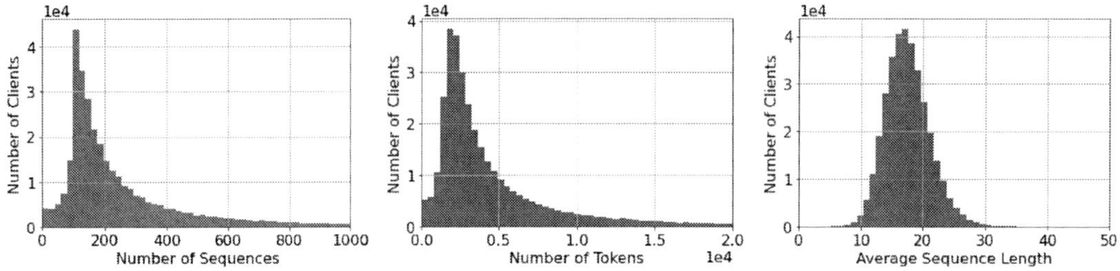

Figure 9: Stack Overflow train split sub-word statistics.

Table 1: Selected architectures for each model and size range. The values in [ ] are the possible hyperparameter values searched over. Layer Size refers to the LSTM layer dimension and MLP layer dimension for Transformer and # Layers refers to number of LSTM layers and number of Transformer blocks.

Model	# Parameters	Embedding Size	Layer Size	# Layers
		$[128, 256, 512, 1024]$	$[512, 1024, 2048]$	$[1, 2, 4, 6, 8]$
Small LSTM	4.7M	256	2048	1
Small Transformer	4.1M	128	2048	6
Large LSTM	18.8M	1024	2048	1
Large Transformer	21.0M	512	2048	6

Table 2: Test metrics after 10K rounds of training for each class of model and number of clients per round. The results in **bold** indicate the best for each size range.

Model	# Clients	Perplexity
Small LSTM	200	35.31
Small LSTM	400	34.93
Small LSTM	800	**34.80**
Small Transformer	200	40.18
Small Transformer	400	39.38
Small Transformer	800	38.66
Large LSTM	200	30.97
Large LSTM	400	30.79
Large LSTM	800	30.83
Large Transformer	200	30.64
Large Transformer	400	29.81
Large Transformer	800	**29.15**

For the baseline architecture search, Table 1 details the selected architectures as well as the search ranges for each dimension. The final hyperparameters were selected based on the test perplexity after 3K rounds of training using FedAvg with 200 clients per round. From here on, we fix the Adam optimizer with β_1 at 0.9, β_2 at 0.999, and epsilon at $1e^{-8}$. Additionally, based on the distribution of average sequence lengths across Stack Overflow clients in Figure 9, we fix the max sequence length for training and evaluation to 30.

Table 2 contains the results for each selected model after 10K rounds of training using FedAvg with 200, 400, and 800 clients per round. As expected, the best results are achieved by using 800 clients per round. Thus, from here on, we report results for 800 clients per round only. For these experiments, we

Table 3: Selected hyperparameters for each model and size range. The values in [ ] are the possible hyperparameter values searched over. Batch Size, # Examples, and Clipnorm here apply to the client local SGD steps. LR is learning rate.

Model	Batch Size	# Examples	Clipnorm	Client LR	Server LR
	$[8, 16]$	$[1200, 1600]$	$[0.0, 16.0]$	$[0.01, 0.1, 0.5, 1.0, 2.0]$	$[0.001, 0.01]$
Small LSTM	16	1200	16.0	1.0	0.001
Small Transformer	16	1200	0.0	0.1	0.001
Large LSTM	16	1200	16.0	1.0	0.001
Large Transformer	16	1200	0.0	0.5	0.001

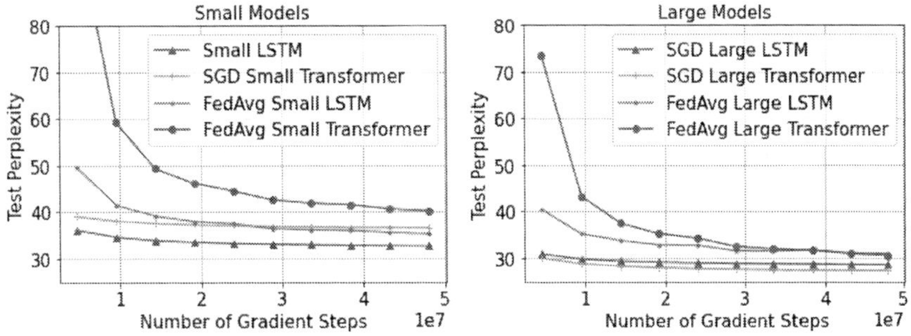

Figure 10: Test set perplexity as a function of number of gradient computations for comparing the centralized and federated averaging baselines.

also search over client learning rate, client batch size, client max number of examples (with client number of epochs fixed to 1), client ℓ_2 norm for clipping, and server learning rate. The search ranges as well as selected values for each model are detailed in Table 3. For all following experiments, we fix client batch size to 16 and client max number of examples to 1200 since the larger batch size consistently performed the best and Figure 9 shows that 1200 sequences is more than enough to cover the vast majority of clients with the number of epochs fixed at 1. We also search over the same ranges for all following experiments where applicable for consistency.

As an additional baseline comparison, we also train each model using synchronous SGD to observe model quality in terms of number of gradient computations. These centralized baselines provide a rough estimate of an upper bound on model quality for federated learning. To produce a reasonable comparison between the federated and centralized experiments, we compare by number of gradient computations. We approximate the number of gradient steps taken for federated learning with 200 clients per round for 10K communication rounds. We train the centralized models using the Adam optimizer and run periodic evaluation on the test set at the same frequency as the federated experiments. We report and compare final metrics between centralized training and federated averaging on the test set in Figure 10. Observing the test perplexity over gradient steps, it is evident that the relative rankings of the models remain consistent between centralized and federated baselines. Additionally, by 10K rounds, the large federated models seem to approach somewhat close in perplexity to their centralized counterparts.

B Partial model training

In our experiments with PVT, we vary the percentage of trainable variables from 10% to 90% in increments of 10. As before, we search over the hyperparameters in Table 3 and find them to be mostly consistent with baseline other than client learning rate. Following Yang et al. (2021), we use the per client per round (PCPR) configuration, where the frozen variables vary from round to round and from client to client, as this was shown to achieve the highest accuracy. Specifically, we only freeze subsets of the multiplicative vectors and matrices of the original model. This corresponds to the embedding and weights of the LSTM, and for the Transformer, the weights of the MLP layer, attention matrices, layer normalization in each

Table 4: Test perplexity after 10K communication rounds of training for each class of model and PVT % of trainable variables.

Model	Trainable %	# Parameters	Perplexity
Small LSTM	100%	4.7M	34.80
Small Transformer	100%	4.1M	38.66
Large LSTM	100%	18.8M	30.83
Large LSTM	40%	7.5M	31.53
Large LSTM	20%	3.8M	32.93
Large Transformer	100%	21.0M	29.15
Large Transformer	40%	8.4M	30.45
Large Transformer	20%	4.2M	32.61

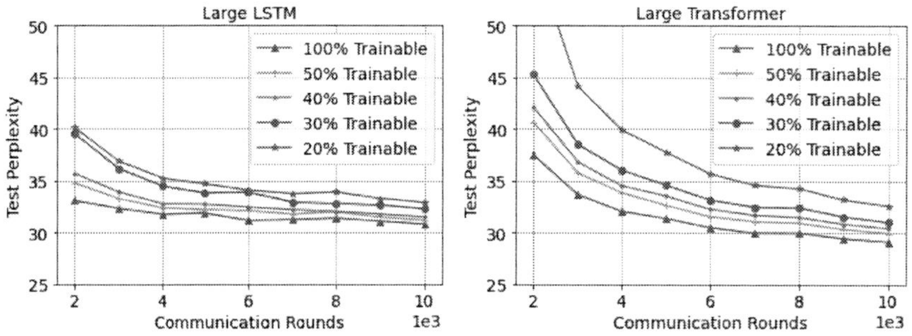

Figure 11: Test perplexity over communication rounds for the large models with select percentages of trainable variables denoted by $X\%$ with 100% indicating all trainable variables are trained (i.e. baseline).

block, and embedding. We also note though that although overall the number of trainable variables might average to the desired percentage (e.g. 10%), for certain architectures, like LSTM, that don't have that many *freezable variables* (only one layer's weight matrix and embedding matrix), the number of trained variables will be much more variable from round to round. On the other hand, for architectures, like Transformer, that have more freezable variables (6 blocks' weight matrices and attention matrices and embeddings), the number of trained is much more consistent between rounds.

We report test set perplexity over communication rounds for the large architectures and varying degrees of PVT in Figure 11 with the number of clients per round set to 800. Looking at Table 4, it is evident that both large models can handle some percentage of partial freezing up until a certain point and that the Large Transformer with only 40% of trainable variables can reach a similar perplexity as the Large LSTM with 100% trainable variables by 10K rounds or so. However, training for the full 10K rounds can be a communication bottleneck so PVT would need to be combined with another technique to reduce the number of rounds needed.

C Quantization

In stochastic k-level uniform quantization (Suresh et al., 2017), values in each layer are converted into one of k evenly distributed values between the layer min and max, stochastically assigned to the closest target value either above or below the real value. The lower the k value, the more the data is being compressed, as the number of bits used to store the value equals $\log_2(k)$. For download quantization, we explore k values corresponding to between 8 and 28 bits. For upload quantization, which can be a larger bottleneck in edge devices (Statista.com, 2021), we explore k values corresponding to between 1 and 28 bits. On upload, we also try applying zero-centering during uniform quantization as well as trying the TernGrad (Wen et al., 2017) algorithm, which quantizes values in each vector v into only one of three values, 0 and $\pm\max(|v|)$, corresponding to $\log_2(3)$ (~ 1.585) bits per parameter. While TernGrad is designed to use L infinity clipping (ℓ_∞), we experiment with and without this for completeness.

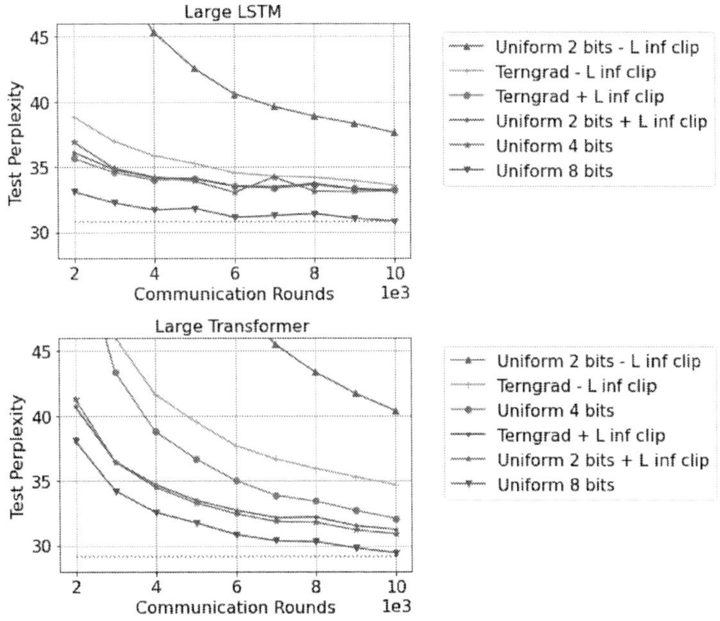

Figure 12: Test set perplexity over communication rounds for varying upload quantization levels, with download quantization fixed to 16 bits. The dotted line shows baseline perplexity achieved after 10K rounds without any quantization.

While ℓ_∞ clipping did make a significant difference in the TernGrad experiment for Transformers, performing much better with it than without, it did not have a large effect on the TernGrad performance in the LSTM in Figure 12. TernGrad and its counterpart uniform quantization to ~ 1.585 bits performed the same, as long as ℓ_∞ clipping was applied. It is clear from the uniform 2-bit experiments as well that ℓ_∞ clipping is important when quantizing into these lower number of bits; the 2-bit experiment without clipping performs much worse than the Terngrad without clipping, although enabling clipping allows 2-bit to perform slightly better than Terngrad's $\log_2(3)$ bits with clipping. Zero-centering did not seem to affect upload behavior much for either model, marginally improving the LSTM and marginally degrading the Transformer.

We explore the patterns of communication cost for each experiment setting in Figure 5. We calculate the approximate download and upload MB for each experiment by multiplying the model's number of parameters by the number of download or upload bits to get total bits transported.

Examining Figure 5, we note the baseline points for each set of experiments as the lowest and rightmost, getting the best perplexity but also highest communication cost. Starting from there, we see trends of no perplexity degradation as we apply conservative quantization to the Large LSTM and Transformer settings and move left in the plot. We then reach an elbow in the points for each setting right around where the Terngrad point is, from which point perplexity degrades drastically without much communication cost savings as the points head up in two lines as upload quantization is reduced, with one line corresponding to experiments with download 16 bits and the other to download 12 bits. While the Terngrad point for the Large Transformer falls at the outermost point in the "elbow" and therefore gives the best tradeoff for cost versus perplexity, there is one uniform quantization point that does better than the Large LSTM Terngrad, which is download 12 bits and upload 6 bits. It makes sense that this does well as we saw that the LSTM was able to use these settings without much regression from the baseline performance, while the Transformer could only quantize to 16 download bits and 8 upload bits without regressions.

Table 5: Selected hyperparameters for each centrally trained model and dataset. The values in [ ] are the possible hyperparameter values searched over.

Model	Dataset	Clipnorm $[0, 16]$	Learning Rate $[1e^{-5}, 5e^{-5}, 1e^{-4}, 5e^{-4}, 1e^{-3}, 5e^{-3}, 1e^{-2}]$
Small LSTM	Book	16.0	$5e^{-5}$
Small LSTM	LM1B	0.0	$5e^{-5}$
Large LSTM	Book	0.0	$5e^{-5}$
Large LSTM	LM1B	0.0	$5e^{-5}$
Small Transformer	Book	0.0	$1e^{-4}$
Small Transformer	LM1B	16.0	$1e^{-4}$
Large Transformer	Book	16.0	$5e^{-5}$
Large Transformer	LM1B	16.0	$5e^{-5}$

D Transfer learning

To find the best models pretrained on the Books and LM1B datasets, we train for 30M steps of synchronous SGD searching over learning rate and clip norm. Like our other centrally trained models, the batch size is fixed to 16 and Adam is used with β_1 at 0.9, β_2 at 0.999, and epsilon at $1e^{-8}$. See Table 5 for the selected hyperparameters.

Next we warmstart each models with the parameters from the best corresponding pretrained centralized model and train using FedAvg for 10K rounds. We sweep over clip norm and client learning rate. See Table 6 for the selected hyperparameters. Clip norm is omitted in Table 6, since for all hyperparameter sweeps 16 was the best value. The Book dataset outperforms the LM1B dataset in all model architectures across LSTM and Transformer. Investigating the difference between the two datasets and their similarities to the Stackoverflow dataset to determine why Books always outperformed LM1B remains an interesting open question.

E Different optimizers

In an effort to improve communication efficiency of the larger language models, we examine two communication-efficient federated algorithms: MimeLite and FedProx. By comparing the speed and point of convergence of these algorithms in number of rounds, we can determine if the overall communication cost of training can be decreased. As before, we fix the model architectures for each class of model and conduct a basic search over learning hyperparameters using the same common search space as Table 3 with the addition of the following algorithm specific hyperparameter sweeps. For MimeLite, we use Adagrad (Duchi et al., 2011) for the base optimizer as this setup was shown to perform the best by Karimireddy et al. (2020) for Stack Overflow. For the MimeLite Adagrad base optimizer, we sweep over base learning rates of $[0.01, 0.03, 0.1, 0.3, 1.0]$ and epsilons of $[1e^{-1}, 1e^{-3}, 1e^{-5}, 1e^{-7}]$ and fix the server learning rate to 1.0. For FedProx, we sweep over μ values of $[0, 0.1, 0.01, 0.001, 0.0001]$ which controls the weight of the L2 squared norm.

We report test perplexity over 10K federated training rounds with 800 clients per round in Figure 7 and Table 7. While FedProx does slightly outperform FedAvg, it does not significantly alter the speed of training in terms of number of communication rounds. Thus, we chose to continue using FedAvg in the combination experiments for consistency across experiments and more accurate comparisons.

F Combination of techniques

For the combination experiments, we conducted a joint search over a smaller range of hyperparameters for each technique to keep the total search space reasonable. For PVT, we restricted the possible percentages to 20%, 30%, and 40% of trainable variables as those were shown to yield good performance while cutting model size to less than half the original size. For uniform quantization, we restricted the search of

Table 6: Test set metrics after 10K communication rounds of training for each class of model and pretrain dataset. The client learning rate listed is the best performing learning rate found from a hyperparameter sweep.Reported Δ metrics are the change in quality relative to Table 2.

Model	Dataset	# Clients	Client Learning Rate [0.01, 0.1, 0.5, 1.0, 2.0]	Δ Perplexity
Small LSTM	Book	200	1.0	0.24
Small LSTM	Book	400	0.5	1.09
Small LSTM	Book	800	0.5	1.66
Small LSTM	LM1B	200	1.0	0.53
Small LSTM	LM1B	400	0.5	1.72
Small LSTM	LM1B	800	0.5	2.36
Large LSTM	Book	200	0.5	0.59
Large LSTM	Book	400	0.1	0.79
Large LSTM	Book	800	0.5	0.94
Large LSTM	LM1B	200	0.5	0.91
Large LSTM	LM1B	400	0.1	1.09
Large LSTM	LM1B	800	0.5	1.3
Small Transformer	Book	200	0.1	0.35
Small Transformer	Book	400	0.1	1.83
Small Transformer	Book	800	0.1	3.34
Small Transformer	LM1B	200	0.1	0.42
Small Transformer	LM1B	400	0.1	1.97
Small Transformer	LM1B	800	0.1	3.49
Large Transformer	Book	200	0.5	**−1.92**
Large Transformer	Book	400	0.1	**−0.76**
Large Transformer	Book	800	0.1	**−0.04**
Large Transformer	LM1B	200	0.1	**−1.81**
Large Transformer	LM1B	400	0.1	**−0.64**
Large Transformer	LM1B	800	0.1	0.14

upload to 6 or 8 bits and download to 16 or 32 bits since the Transformer was shown to be able to handle aggressive upload quantization but required more care on download quantization. Finally, for transfer learning, we warmstarted after pretraining on the Books corpus. As in previous experiments, we also search over the common hyperparameter space defined in Table 3, where applicable.

Similar to previous experiments, we use 800 clients per round and train for 10K rounds with FedAvg. Figure 13 and Table 8 contain the results for the large models with and without the efficient techniques applied. We apply two levels of quantization on download, 16 and 32 bits, and observe that the Large LSTM is more amenable to download quantization compared to the Large Transformer as the regression between the two levels is much smaller for the LSTM than the Transformer. However, the Transformer with 16 bit download quantization still outperforms all efficient LSTMs though it requires more communication rounds to do so than the efficient Transformer with 32 bits for download. For the remaining analysis, we focus on the efficient Transformer using 32 bits for download. It is clear that for the Large Transformer, applying efficient techniques yields better quality in earlier communication rounds. Although there are regressions in the final model quality after 10K rounds of training, this could be attributed to previously observed issues with increased amounts of labeled data diminishing the value pretraining (Zoph et al., 2020). However, the Efficient Large Transformer still reaches the same final perplexity as the Large LSTM which had no efficient techniques applied. Furthermore, when considered in terms of actual communication cost, as is done in Figure 8, the efficient models yield much better performance at smaller total communication costs.

Table 7: Test perplexity after 10K communication rounds of training for each class of model and federated algorithm.

Model	Algorithm	Perplexity
Small LSTM	FedAvg	34.80
Small LSTM	MimeLite	34.81
Small LSTM	FedProx	34.66
Small Transformer	FedAvg	38.66
Small Transformer	MimeLite	39.88
Small Transformer	FedProx	38.57
Large LSTM	FedAvg	30.83
Large LSTM	MimeLite	31.00
Large LSTM	FedProx	30.76
Large Transformer	FedAvg	29.15
Large Transformer	MimeLite	30.39
Large Transformer	FedProx	29.04

Table 8: Test perplexity and total communication costs in gigabytes after 10K communication rounds of training for each class of model and setup. If the number of download bits is unspecified, the standard 32 bits was used.

Model	Download Cost (GB)	Upload Cost (GB)	Perplex.
Small LSTM	188	188	34.80
Small Transformer	164	164	38.66
Large LSTM	752	752	30.83
Large Transformer	840	840	29.15
Efficient Large LSTM (download 32 bits)	752	75	32.57
Efficient Large Transformer (download 32 bits)	840	84	30.83
Efficient Large LSTM (download 16 bits)	376	75	32.76
Efficient Large Transformer (download 16 bits)	420	84	32.32

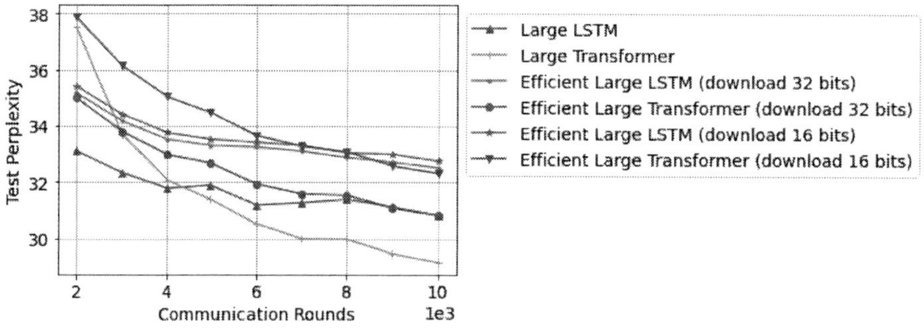

Figure 13: Test perplexity over communication rounds for the large models with and without efficient techniques applied.

Adaptive Differential Privacy for Language Modeling

Xinwei Wu[1]†, Li Gong[2], Deyi Xiong[1] *
[1]College of Intelligence and Computing, Tianjin University, Tianjin, China
[2]ByteDance Lark AI, Beijing, China
{wuxw2021,dyxiong}@tju.edu.cn, franck.gong@bytedance.com

Abstract

Although differential privacy (DP) can protect language models from leaking privacy, its indiscriminative protection on all data points reduces its practical utility. Previous works improve DP training by discriminating private and non-private data. But these works rely on datasets with prior privacy information, which is not available in real-world scenarios. In this paper, we propose an **Adaptive Differential Privacy** (ADP) framework for language modeling without resorting to prior privacy information. We estimate the probability that a linguistic item contains privacy based on a language model. We further propose a new Adam algorithm that adjusts the degree of differential privacy noise injected to the language model according to the estimated privacy probabilities. Experiments demonstrate that our ADP improves differentially private language modeling to achieve good protection from canary attackers.

1 Introduction

Language modeling is a foundation problem in natural language processing (Bommasani et al., 2021). Recent large language models (Brown et al., 2020; Zeng et al., 2021) are usually trained at scale. Unfortunately, large language models have a tendency to remember training data in the absence of appropriate privacy protection mechanisms (Carlini et al., 2019, 2021). Since data, which are usually collected from public sources, e.g., tweets, blogs, may contain sensitive information (personal address, SSN numbers, and so on) learning a safe large language model has become increasingly important.

In recent years, differential privacy (Dwork, 2008; Dwork et al., 2014) has become a key privacy preservation method, which attempts to randomize the training algorithm so that the model does not rely too much on any single training instances. Abadi et al. (2016) propose Differential Private Stochastic Gradient Descent (DP-SGD) to protect deep learning models by adding random noise to gradients. However, traditional differential privacy ignores individual attributes of data (McMahan et al., 2018). This overly pessimistic privacy protection results in poor performance or even mis-convergence of training for differentially private language models (Anil et al., 2021). Therefore, approaches are proposed to mitigate this problem by treating private and non-private data separately during the DP training process, such as selective differential privacy (Shi et al., 2021) and sensory-based privacy-χ (Qu et al., 2021). These methods require training data to provide privacy information as a hard label. Unfortunately, it is usually difficult and expensive to manually annotate privacy labels to data. Other studies (Xu et al., 2019; Tesfay et al., 2019) learn to detect privacy information in unstructured texts. However, the prerequisite is knowing keywords or reference texts of privacy information (Neerbek, 2020). Therefore, learning differentially private language models on data without prior privacy information is an open problem yet to be investigated.

In this paper, we propose an **Adaptive Differential Privacy** (ADP) framework without resorting to prior privacy information. The basic assumption behind ADP is that linguistic items containing private information do not occur frequently in real-world texts. Hence, the probability that a linguistic item contains privacy information (hereinafter *privacy probability*) is inversely proportional to the frequency of the linguistic item occurring in the dataset. With this assumption, we can estimate the privacy probability of a linguistic item based on a language model. After estimating these probabilities, we relax the constraint of differential privacy, and propose an adaptive differential privacy

*Corresponding author.
†Work done while this author was an intern at BtyeDance Lark AI.

Proceedings of the First Workshop on Federated Learning for Natural Language Processing (FL4NLP 2022), pages 21 - 26
May 27, 2022 ©2022 Association for Computational Linguistics

method, which adjusts the Guassian noise of differential privacy based on privacy probabilities. To enable this adaptive differential privacy strategy, we further present Adaptive-DP-Adam Algorithm to train differentially private language models.

To evaluate our approach, we train transformer-based language models, and compare the performance of adaptive differential privacy against traditional differential privacy methods. Additionally, we verify the protection effectiveness of ADP models with canary attackers (Carlini et al., 2019). The results suggest that our adaptive differential privacy method can achieve good performance and protection from canary attackers.

The main contributions of this paper are three-fold.

- We propose a method to automatically estimate the probability that a linguistic item contains privacy information, relaxing the requirement of prior privacy information of previous methods.
- A new Adaptive-DP-Adam algorithm is proposed, which adaptively adjusts the magnitude of differential privacy noise to be injected into language models according to privacy probabilities.[1]
- We conduct experiments to validate the effectiveness of the proposed adaptive differential privacy in improving the performance of differentially private models and protecting sensitive information.

2 Related Work

Large language models (Brown et al., 2020; Zhang et al., 2020) have been attracting growing attention. Powerful large language models can achieve substantial improvements on a wide range of downstream NLP tasks. Unfortunately, large language models have a tendency to memorize training data (Carlini et al., 2019). Carlini et al. (2021) have successfully induced GPT-2 (Radford et al., 2019) to output sensitive information in its training data.

Differential privacy (Dwork, 2008; Dwork et al., 2014) is widely used to protect private information of data. Abadi et al. (2016) propose the DP-SGD algorithm to train deep learning models, and apply moment accounting to calculate cumulative privacy loss during training. Although DP-SGD can limit the risk of leaking information from training data, random noise on gradients usually degrades corresponding models (Li et al., 2021), and even cause training to not converge when a large model is trained.

To improve DP-SGD, one way is to change training settings (Li et al., 2021; Hoory et al., 2021), e.g., increasing the batch size or decreasing clipping norm. However, these methods are usually at a higher cost. Other attempts to improve the utilization of dataset information by relaxing the constraints of differential privacy. For example, Ebadi et al. (2015) propose personalized differentiated privacy to provide different levels of privacy protection for different users. Kotsogiannis et al. (2020) develop one-sided differential privacy that only protects sensitive users. Shi et al. (2021) introduce Selective Differential Privacy to add noise only into private data. These methods all need to know which items in the dataset contain private information, which is prohibitively expensive for large-scale datasets. There are some previous works (Xu et al., 2019; Tesfay et al., 2019) detecting sensitive information in unstructured texts, but relying on labeled keywords or reference texts.

3 Preliminary

We will introduce differential privacy (Dwork, 2008; Dwork et al., 2014), and the DP-SGD algorithm (Abadi et al., 2016) as preliminaries in this section.

3.1 Differential Privacy

Intuitively, an algorithm is $(\epsilon; \delta)$-DP if the output of the algorithm cannot be used to probabilistically determine the presence of a single record in the dataset by a factor of e^{ϵ}. Formally, an algorithm A satisfies $(\epsilon; \delta)$-DP if for all datasets $(D_1;D_2)$ that differ from each other by at least one instance, and for any set S, we have $P\{\mathcal{A}(\mathcal{D}_1) \in S\} \leq e^{\epsilon} P\{\mathcal{A}(\mathcal{D}_2) \in S\} + \delta$, where smaller ϵ values indicate a stronger privacy protection.

3.2 DP-SGD Optimization

The basic idea of DP-SGD is to clip each example gradients and add noise during model training.

Specifically, for a batch of size L, the loss function is $\mathcal{L}(\theta) = \frac{1}{L}\sum_{x_i} \mathcal{L}(x_i; \theta)$. For each sample x_i in the batch, the gradient of $g(x_i)$ is first cut using the l_2 norm according to the gradient clipping level C, so that the maximum value of loss does

[1] Code is available at `https://github.com/flamewei123/ADP`.

not exceed C:

$$g(x_i) = \frac{1}{\max\{1, \|\nabla_\theta \mathcal{L}(x_i;\theta)\|_2 / C\}} \nabla_\theta \mathcal{L}(x_i;\theta). \quad (1)$$

For a batch L_t, after the sum of clipping gradients of all samples in L_t is calculated, the Gaussian noise $z \sim \mathcal{N}(0, \sigma^2 C^2 I)$ is added to the sum of gradients. Hence a new gradient $\tilde{g_{L_t}}$ required for back propagation is computed as follows:

$$\tilde{g_{L_t}} = \frac{1}{L}(\textstyle\sum_{x_i} g(x_i) + z_t). \quad (2)$$

The smaller C can lead to more stable training. And a smaller value of σ indicates smaller noise z.

4 Adaptive Differential Privacy

In this section, we will elaborate the proposed **Adaptive Differential Privacy**. First, we introduce a method to evaluate the privacy probability of a linguistic item. Second, we propose an adaptive noise method, which adjusts the noise magnitude according to the privacy probability of an item in DP-SGD process. Finally, an Adam gradient optimization algorithm based on adaptive noise is proposed.

4.1 Privacy Probability Evaluation

The range of privacy is not fixed but relying on its owner, which makes it hard to judge the privacy. To solve this problem, we introduce the following assumption.

Assumption 1: *Texts containing privacy information do not occur frequently in a large dataset.*

We assume that the probability of texts containing private information is related to the frequency of texts appearing in dataset. Hence, the judgment of privacy can be transformed into the evaluation of the text frequency, which means the privacy probability of a token sequence is in direct proportion to the frequency of this sequence.

We then introduce a simple yet effective method to measure the frequency of text based on large-scale pre-trained language models. Giving a token sequence $s = x_1, x_2, ..., x_n$, the perplexity of the sequence is computed as follows:

$$\mathcal{P}(s) = \exp(-\frac{1}{n}\sum_{i=1}^{n} \log f_\theta(x_i|x_1, ..., x_{i-1})). \quad (3)$$

When the perplexity is low, it indicates that the average probability of text prediction is high. Large language models like GPT use a huge amount of text data for training. Hence, we consider such a large language model to be a trustworthy estimator.

The perplexity from a trustworthy language model is inversely proportional to the occurrence frequence of the text $o(s) \propto \frac{1}{\mathcal{P}(s)}$, and the privacy probability of s is proportional to the perplexity of s: $\rho(s) \propto \mathcal{P}(s)$. Based on this, we propose a formula for calculating the privacy probability:

$$\rho(s) = \textbf{normalize}(\mathcal{P}(s)), \quad (4)$$

where $s \in D$ and **normalize** is a normalization operator that transforms values into probability values (i.e., falling between 0 and 1).

The above method that estimates the privacy probability is not precise enough, which will inevitably cause some non-private and long-tail instances to be identified as private samples. However, from the perspective of privacy protection, such a cost is still acceptable.

4.2 Adaptive Noise

During differential privacy training, in the batch $B = s_1, s_2, ..., s_L$ of size L, the privacy probability of a token sequence $s_i \in B$ is $\rho(s_i)$, and the Gaussian noise of B is $z_B = \mathcal{N}(0, C^2\sigma^2 I^2)$, where σ is a noise multiplier, and C is the clipping norm. To improve the target model performance, we introduce the **privacy weight** to change the magnitude of Gaussian noise

$$\gamma_B = \frac{\sum_i^L \rho(s_i)}{L}. \quad (5)$$

The **privacy weight** denotes a privacy probability averaged over batch B. We incorporate it to the Gaussian noise:

$$z_{B_{adp}} = \gamma_B \cdot \mathcal{N}(0, C^2\sigma^2 I^2). \quad (6)$$

Through this method, we adaptively change the noise of every batch according to its privacy weight.

4.3 Adaptive DP Optimization

With the adaptive noise, we further develop a privacy mechanism to train models. Abadi et al. (2016) propose DP-SGD that adds Gaussian noise to gradients and applies stochastic gradient descent (SGD) to train private deep learning models. We incorporate our proposed adaptive noise into DP-SGD.

Such adapted framework is also suitable for other optimization algorithms such as Adam. The whole procedure of Adaptive-DP-Adam is described in **Algorithm 1**.

Algorithm 1: Adaptive-DP-Adam

Input: dataset $D = \{x_i\}_{i=1}^{N}$, a large language model f_{LM}, loss function $L(\theta)$

Parameters: learning rate η, noise level σ, batch B of size L, clipping norm C, step E, Adam parameters $\{\theta_0, m_0, m_1, \delta_1, \delta_2\}$

```
Let G(φ) = 0
for all t ∈ T do
    Sample a batch B_t, with sampling probability L/N
    Calculate γ_{B_t} based on Eq. (5)
    for all x_i ∈ B_t do
        Clip gradients
        g̃_t(x_i) ← g_t(x_i) · min(1, C/ ||g_t(x_i)||_2)
    end for
    Generate adaptive noise z_t based on Eq. (6)
    Calculate average gradients
    ḡ_t(x_i) = (1/L)(z_t + Σ_{i=1}^{L} g̃_t(x_i))
    Update parameters θ using usual Adam
end for
return θ_T
```

5 Experiments

5.1 Settings

Dataset We used Wikitext-103 (Merity et al., 2016) to train our model, which is a widely used dataset for language modeling from a set of verified Good and Featured articles on Wikipedia.

Baselines We have two baselines, one without DP (denoted by "No-DP"), and the other trained with DP-SGD (denoted by "DP-SGD"). We refer to our models trained with ADP-SGD as "ADP".

Hyper-parameters We used a 12-layer transformer decoder to train the language model with hidden size of 1024 and batch size of 4096, training 20 epoches with inital learning rate of 5×10^{-5}. The clipping norm C was set to 0.001, and the noise multiplier σ was 1 or 5.

5.2 Canary Attacker

Canary insertion is proposed by Carlini et al. (2019), which inserts random sequences called canaries into the training dataset and calculates the exposure for the inserted canaries during testing to measure whether the model memorizes these canaries. In our setting, we injected "My ID is 955320" into the Wikitext-103 dataset for 10, 100, and 1000 times to make the differences between

model	test loss	test PPL	sigma	epsilon
No-DP	7.08	256.66	-	-
DP-SGD	13.08	7582.65	1.0	4.22
ADP	**12.65**	**4426.05**	1.0	6.35
No-DP	7.08	256.66	-	-
DP-SGD	17.65	20815.23	5.0	0.1
ADP	**14.85**	**8635.66**	5.0	2.47

Table 1: The performance of language models trained by our method and baselines. We compare results by varying the noise level σ.

models more salient. Given a canary $s[r]$, and a model with parameters θ, the exposure of $s[r]$ is calculated as:

$$\mathbf{exposure} = \log_2 |\mathcal{R}| - \log_2 \mathbf{rank}_\theta(s[r]), \quad (7)$$

where $\mathcal{R}$ is the set of all possible results, and $\mathbf{rank}(s[r])$ is the position of $s[r]$ in $\mathcal{R}$. The lower the exposure, the safer the model is.

5.3 Results

Model Performance We first evaluated models trained by different privacy settings on language modeling task. Both models were trained using a transformer decoder architecture. As shown in Table 1, DP-SGD performs poorly, and larger noise σ further worses the model. In contrast, our ADP helps model to alleviate the decaying performance, and the utility grows when the noise multiplier σ is large. Although the privacy guarantee ϵ of ADP increases compared to DP-SGD when the noise multiplier σ is 1 and 5, the privacy guarantee of ADP is within the acceptable range. It suggests that our ADP can improve the performance of differentially private language models with tight privacy guarantee.

Protection Against Attacker Our second group of experiments, described in section 5.2, is to test the model memorization of private information. We evaluated models trained on the Wikitext-103 dataset injected canaries. We used text generation to evaluate the exposure of canaries from different language models. As can be seen from Figure 1, even when private item appears as many as 1000 times in the data, the ADP model performs significantly better than the non-DP model. However, exposures of the ADP model are larger than the DP-SGD model. It suggests that ADP method can protect privacy information from leaking from training data, but the protection performance is slightly worse than DP-SGD.

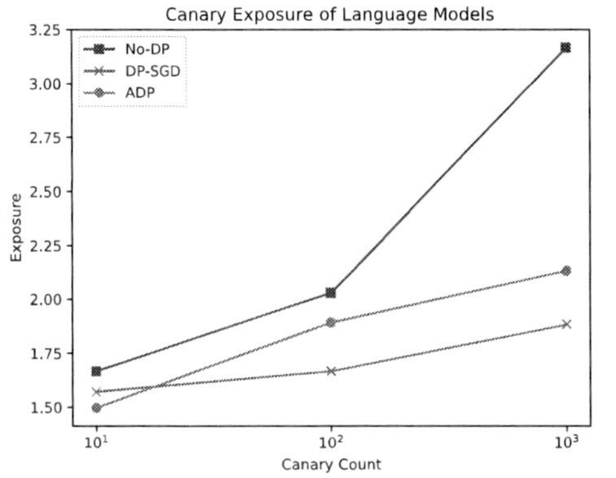

Figure 1: The exposure of canaries from different language models. All models were trained for 20 epoches.

6 Conclusion

We have presented a new method to estimate the privacy probability of a linguistic item when the privacy information of the dataset is not known. With estimated privacy probabilities, we propose adaptive differential privacy (ADP), to improve the model utility. We also present a privacy optimization algorithm, Adaptive-DP-Adam, to train differentially private models. Our experiments show that models trained with ADP achieve better utilities than traditional DP and are capable of protecting sensitive information from being leaked.

Acknowledgements

The work was partially supported by a ByteDance Research Collaboration Project (PJ20210625900030) and the Natural Science Foundation of Tianjin (Grant No. 19JCZDJC31400). We would like to thank the anonymous reviewers for their insightful comments.

References

Martin Abadi, Andy Chu, Ian Goodfellow, H Brendan McMahan, Ilya Mironov, Kunal Talwar, and Li Zhang. 2016. Deep learning with differential privacy. In *Proceedings of the 2016 ACM SIGSAC conference on computer and communications security*, pages 308–318.

Rohan Anil, Badih Ghazi, Vineet Gupta, Ravi Kumar, and Pasin Manurangsi. 2021. Large-scale differentially private bert. *arXiv preprint arXiv:2108.01624*.

Rishi Bommasani, Drew A Hudson, Ehsan Adeli, Russ Altman, Simran Arora, Sydney von Arx, Michael S Bernstein, Jeannette Bohg, Antoine Bosselut, Emma Brunskill, et al. 2021. On the opportunities and risks of foundation models. *https://openreview.net/forum?id=NTs-olaO6O*.

Tom Brown, Benjamin Mann, Nick Ryder, Melanie Subbiah, Jared D Kaplan, Prafulla Dhariwal, Arvind Neelakantan, Pranav Shyam, Girish Sastry, Amanda Askell, et al. 2020. Language models are few-shot learners. *Advances in neural information processing systems*, 33:1877–1901.

Nicholas Carlini, Chang Liu, Úlfar Erlingsson, Jernej Kos, and Dawn Song. 2019. The secret sharer: Evaluating and testing unintended memorization in neural networks. In *28th USENIX Security Symposium (USENIX Security 19)*, pages 267–284.

Nicholas Carlini, Florian Tramer, Eric Wallace, Matthew Jagielski, Ariel Herbert-Voss, Katherine Lee, Adam Roberts, Tom Brown, Dawn Song, Ulfar Erlingsson, et al. 2021. Extracting training data from large language models. In *30th USENIX Security Symposium (USENIX Security 21)*, pages 2633–2650.

Cynthia Dwork. 2008. Differential privacy: A survey of results. In *International conference on theory and applications of models of computation*, pages 1–19. Springer.

Cynthia Dwork, Aaron Roth, et al. 2014. The algorithmic foundations of differential privacy. *Found. Trends Theor. Comput. Sci.*, 9(3-4):211–407.

Hamid Ebadi, David Sands, and Gerardo Schneider. 2015. Differential privacy: Now it's getting personal. *Acm Sigplan Notices*, 50(1):69–81.

Shlomo Hoory, Amir Feder, Avichai Tendler, Sofia Erell, Alon Peled-Cohen, Itay Laish, Hootan Nakhost, Uri Stemmer, Ayelet Benjamini, Avinatan Hassidim, et al. 2021. Learning and evaluating a differentially private pre-trained language model. In *Findings of the Association for Computational Linguistics: EMNLP 2021*, pages 1178–1189.

Ios Kotsogiannis, Stelios Doudalis, Sam Haney, Ashwin Machanavajjhala, and Sharad Mehrotra. 2020. One-sided differential privacy. In *2020 IEEE 36th International Conference on Data Engineering (ICDE)*, pages 493–504. IEEE.

Xuechen Li, Florian Tramer, Percy Liang, and Tatsunori Hashimoto. 2021. Large language models can be strong differentially private learners. *https://openreview.net/forum?id=bVuP3ltATMz*.

H Brendan McMahan, Daniel Ramage, Kunal Talwar, and Li Zhang. 2018. Learning differentially private recurrent language models. In *International Conference on Learning Representations*.

Stephen Merity, Caiming Xiong, James Bradbury, and Richard Socher. 2016. Pointer sentinel mixture models. *https://openreview.net/forum?id=Byj72udxe*.

Jan Neerbek. 2020. *Sensitive Information Detection: Recursive Neural Networks for Encoding Context.* Ph.D. thesis, Aarhus University.

Chen Qu, Weize Kong, Liu Yang, Mingyang Zhang, Michael Bendersky, and Marc Najork. 2021. Natural language understanding with privacy-preserving bert. In *Proceedings of the 30th ACM International Conference on Information & Knowledge Management*, pages 1488–1497.

Alec Radford, Jeffrey Wu, Rewon Child, David Luan, Dario Amodei, Ilya Sutskever, et al. 2019. Language models are unsupervised multitask learners. *OpenAI blog*, 1(8):9.

Weiyan Shi, Aiqi Cui, Evan Li, Ruoxi Jia, and Zhou Yu. 2021. Selective differential privacy for language modeling. *arXiv preprint arXiv:2108.12944.*

Welderufael B Tesfay, Jetzabel Serna, and Kai Rannenberg. 2019. Privacybot: Detecting privacy sensitive information in unstructured texts. In *2019 Sixth International Conference on Social Networks Analysis, Management and Security (SNAMS)*, pages 53–60. IEEE.

Guosheng Xu, Chunhao Qi, Hai Yu, Shengwei Xu, Chunlu Zhao, and Jing Yuan. 2019. Detecting sensitive information of unstructured text using convolutional neural network. In *2019 International Conference on Cyber-Enabled Distributed Computing and Knowledge Discovery (CyberC)*, pages 474–479. IEEE.

Wei Zeng, Xiaozhe Ren, Teng Su, Hui Wang, Yi Liao, Zhiwei Wang, Xin Jiang, ZhenZhang Yang, Kaisheng Wang, Xiaoda Zhang, et al. 2021. Pangu: Large-scale autoregressive pretrained chinese language models with auto-parallel computation. *https://openreview.net/forum?id=-AArJ2Qrh38.*

Zachariah Zhang, Jingshu Liu, and Narges Razavian. 2020. BERT-XML: Large scale automated ICD coding using BERT pretraining. In *Proceedings of the 3rd Clinical Natural Language Processing Workshop*, pages 24–34, Online. Association for Computational Linguistics.

Intrinsic Gradient Compression for Scalable and Efficient Federated Learning

Luke Melas-Kyriazi*
Oxford University
Oxford, UK

Franklyn Wang*
Harvard University
Cambridge, MA

Abstract

Federated learning is a rapidly growing area of research, holding the promise of privacy-preserving distributed training on edge devices. The largest barrier to wider adoption of federated learning is the communication cost of model updates, which is accentuated by the fact that many edge devices are bandwidth-constrained. At the same time, within the machine learning theory community, a separate line of research has emerged around optimizing networks within a subspace of the full space of all parameters. The dimension of the smallest subspace for which these methods still yield strong results is called the *intrinsic dimension*. In this work, we prove a general correspondence between the notions of intrinsic dimension and gradient compressibility, and we show that a family of low-bandwidth federated learning algorithms, which we call *intrinsic gradient compression algorithms*, naturally emerges from this correspondence. Finally, we conduct large-scale NLP experiments using transformer models with over 100M parameters (GPT-2 and BERT), and show that our method outperforms the state-of-the-art in gradient compression.

1 Introduction

Federated learning is a nascent area of study which seeks to perform machine learning in a privacy-preserving way. However, federated learning with deep neural networks suffers from a problem with communication bandwidth: it is very costly to send gradient/model updates over a network, especially when communicating with mobile phones and edge devices.

To reduce bandwidth for federated learning, it is natural to utilize various forms of compression. Previous works have tried to achieve compression in two ways: (1) by compressing the information communicated in standard gradient descent algorithms (e.g. quantizing gradients (Wen et al., 2017)) and (2) by training with non-standard methods that naturally use less bandwidth (e.g. prototypical networks (Tan et al., 2021)).

At the same time, in the machine learning theory community, researchers have been working to understand what at first seems like an entirely different question: why do hugely overparametrized models generalize so well? One promising approach to this answering this question has utilized the concept of *intrinsic dimension*, defined for a given optimization problem as the smallest dimension d for which we can solve the problem when the weights are restricted to a a d-dimensional manifold. To be precise, it is the smallest d for which the standard loss minimization problem

$$\min_{\theta' \in \mathbb{R}^d} \ell(f_{g(\theta')}) \quad (1)$$

has a satisfactory solution, where the image of g is a d-dimensional manifold. If the intrinsic dimension of a problem is low, then even if a model is vastly overparameterized, only a small number of parameters need to be tuned in order to obtain a good solution, which is often enough to imply certain generalization guarantees.

We begin this paper by observing that the two problems above are naturally related. If one can find a solution to the problem by only tuning d parameters, as in Equation (1), then a corresponding low bandwidth algorithm can be found by simply running stochastic gradient descent in the reduced parameter space (in this case, $\mathbb{R}^d$).

However, simply optimizing a subset of a model's parameters is often insufficient for training models (especially when training from scratch, rather than finetuning). Thus, we are inspired to seek a more general characterization of algorithms that use a low amount of bandwidth. In order to do this, we rewrite the optimization problem in Equation (1) in the original parameter space. When $g(\theta') = A\theta'$ for some matrix A (so the low-dimensional manifold is a low-dimensional sub-

* Equal contribution

Proceedings of the First Workshop on Federated Learning for Natural Language Processing (FL4NLP 2022), pages 27 - 41
May 27, 2022

space), stochastic gradient descent can be rewritten as

$$\theta_{t+1} = \theta_t - \eta A A^\top \nabla_\theta \ell(f_\theta)|_{\theta=\theta_t}. \quad (2)$$

We call this method *static intrinsic gradient compression*, because our gradients are projected into a static ("intrinsic") subspace. Now, Equation (2) admits a natural generalization, which allows us to explore more of the parameter space while still preserving a low level of upload bandwidth usage:

$$\theta_{t+1} = \theta_t - \eta A_t A_t^\top \nabla_\theta \ell(f_\theta)|_{\theta=\theta_t} \quad (3)$$

where A_t may vary with time. We call the set of all such algorithms *intrinsic gradient compression algorithms*, and consider three particular instantiations: static, time-varying, and k-varying, each of which perform in different use cases.

Our approach is model-agnostic and highly scalable. In experiments across multiple federated learning benchmarks (language modeling, text classification, and image classification), we vastly outperform prior gradient compression methods, and show strong performance even at very high compression rates (e.g. up to 1000×).

Our contributions are as follows.

- We find a general class of optimization algorithms based on the notion of intrinsic dimension that use low amounts of upload bandwidth, which we denote *intrinsic gradient compression algorithms*.
- We specify three such algorithms: static compression, time-varying compression and K-varying compression, with different levels of upload and download bandwidth for use in various federated settings.
- In a set of experiments, we show that these methods significantly outperform prior approaches to federated learning with gradient compression, obtaining large reductions in bandwidth at the same level of performance.

In Section 2, we describe the preliminaries needed to contextualize our work, namely ideas from intrinsic dimension, federated learning, and gradient compression. In Section 3, we show how the algorithm used by intrinsic dimension naturally generalizes to algorithms which use little upload bandwidth. In Section 4 we consider special instantiations of these algorithms in federated learning settings which attain low upload and download bandwidth, and in Section 5 show that they achieve state of the art results. Finally, Section 6 concludes.

2 Preliminaries

2.1 Intrinsic Dimension

The concept of intrinsic dimension was introduced in the work of (Li et al., 2018), as a way of evaluating the true difficulty of an optimization problem. While this can usually be done by counting the number of parameters, some optimization problems are easier than others in that solutions may be far more plentiful.. One can write

$$\ell(f_\theta) = \ell(f_{g(\theta')}) \quad (4)$$

where $g : \mathbb{R}^d \to \mathbb{R}^D$ and thus we've transformed the problem into an optimization problem over θ_2. If we can still find good solutions to the original problem where $\theta_2 \in \Theta^2$, then the problem's intrinsic dimension may be lower, and thus the question may be easier than previously expected. Throughout this paper we will always take $g(\theta') = A\theta' + \theta_0$ for a $D \times d$ matrix A, and take $\Theta^2 = \mathbb{R}^d$, and $\Theta^1 = \mathbb{R}^D$, where $D > d$, where θ_0 is the original value of the expression.

The intrinisic dimension $g(\ell, L)$ with respect to a task ℓ and performance threshold L is equal to the smallest integer d so that optimizing Equation (4) on task ℓ could lead to a solution of performance at least equal to T. The intrinsic dimension is not exactly knowable, because we cannot find the "best performing model" exactly. However, if say, training with some optimization algorithm gives us a solution to Equation (4) with loss $\leq L$ and with d dimensions, we can say with certainty that $g(\ell, T) \leq d$.

2.2 Federated Learning

Federated learning is a paradigm built around protecting the privacy of user data. The standard model involves a server and many clients, where the raw data must remain on the client's device but the server learns a model. Generally, this is implemented by only the gradients of the model on the data being sent to the central server, which then runs a standard algorithm. A common example of this is the FedAvg algorithm (McMahan et al., 2017), where models are trained to near-completion on a each client's data, and the data is then averaged. In what follows, we define an *epoch* to be a single pass over every client.

2.3 Gradient Compression

Sending full gradients in standard uncompressed form uses far more bandwidth than we are afforded in certain settings. For example, in a 1 billion parameter model (hardly particularly large by current standards) one gradient update would take 4 gigabytes of bandwidth uncompressed. Thus, there has been substantial amounts of work in compressing the gradient, like (Albasyoni et al., 2020), which finds an optimal gradient compression algorithm, albeit one which is computationally infeasible.

2.4 Related Work: Model Pruning and Model Compression

Related Work: Model Pruning There has been great interest in compressing models by using fewer weights, starting with the work of (Hinton et al., 2015; Han et al., 2015). One related work is *Diff Pruning* (Guo et al., 2021), which constrains the number of weights that can be changed from a pretrained model. In essence, diff pruning attempts to solve an L^0 minimization problem on the weights of the model, and approaches this by means of a relaxation.

A number of other works have explored the idea of finetuning by only modifying a subset of a model's parameters. (Jiang et al., 2019) and (Bibikar et al., 2021) utilize sparsity to reduce communication costs during training. (Ravfogel et al., 2021) finetunes only the layer biases of large models. Similarly, (Houlsby et al., 2019) finetunes low-parameter adapters between each layer. Compared to (Ravfogel et al., 2021) our method is far more flexible, allowing any number of parameters to be changed. Compared to (Houlsby et al., 2019) our methods are architecture-independent, and can be applied to any model.

Related Work: Federated Learning Federated learning is a machine learning paradigm in which a model is trained by a collection of clients, each with their own private local data. From the introduction of federated learning (McMahan et al., 2017), it was clear that communication costs represented a significant challenge: sending gradients or weights over a network is costly due to the large size of modern machine learning models. (McMahan et al., 2017) introduced the FedAvg algorithm, which aims to reduce communication costs by sending and averaging weights, rather than gradients. Specifically, clients train their model locally for a given number of epochs, send it to the server, and received an averaged copy of the model weights. However, sending the full set of model weights often remains very costly (especially when clients only have a small amount of local data, such that many rounds of communication are necessary); as a result, FedAvg performs poorly in heavily-bandwidth-constrained settings.

Recently, FetchSGD (Rothchild et al., 2020) aimed to address this issue differently by utilizing the concept of sketching. Rather than transmitting full gradients from the client to the server, they send a sketch of the gradient. This approach performs well, but only yields moderate compression rates. We compare to FetchSGD in Section 5.

3 A Family of Low-Bandwidth Algorithms

In this section, we characterize a family of low-bandwidth optimization algorithms based on the notion of intrinsic dimension.

We start from the optimization problem induced by intrinsic dimension (Equation (4)). If we directly run gradient descent on Equation (4) with respect to the intrinsic weights θ', we obtain an equation of the following form:

$$\theta'_{t+1} = \theta'_t - \eta \nabla_{\theta'} \left(\ell(f_{g(\theta')})\right) = \theta'_t - \eta \nabla_{\theta'} \left(\ell(f_{A\theta'}\right.$$
$$= \theta'_t - \eta A^\top \nabla_\theta (\ell(f_\theta))^\top |_{\theta = A\theta'_t + \theta_0}$$

Then, left-multiplying both sides by A we obtain

$$\theta_{t+1} = \theta_t - \eta \underbrace{A \underbrace{A^\top \nabla_\theta (\ell(f_\theta))|_{\theta=\theta_t}}_{\text{compressed gradient}}}_{\text{approximate gradient}} \tag{5}$$

Note that here, we can interpret $A^\top \nabla_\theta(\ell(f(\theta)))|_{\theta=\theta_t}$ as a compressed gradient with dimension d, and $AA^\top \nabla_\theta(\ell(f(\theta)))|_{\theta=\theta_t}$ as the approximate gradient. This inspires us to consider the more general family of optimization algorithms given by

$$\theta_{t+1} = \theta_t - \eta A_t A_t^\top (\boldsymbol{v}_t), \tag{6}$$

where $\boldsymbol{v}_t$ is a D dimensional vector computed from data available at timestep t that plays a similar role to a gradient, but may not be an exact gradient, and the A_t are all $D \times d$ matrices known ahead of time (say, generated with random seeds). One intuitive way of interpreting this algorithm is that $\theta_{t+1} - \theta_t$ is constrained to lie in a low-dimensional subspace,

Algorithm 1 Static Intrinsic Gradient Compression

input: learning rate η, timesteps T, local batch size ℓ, clients per round W
Create matrix $A \in \mathbb{R}^{D \times d}$ with $\mathbb{E}[AA^\top] = I_D$.
Current Vector: $\Sigma_0 = 0$
for $t = 1, 2 \cdots T$ **do**
  Randomly select W clients $c_1, \ldots c_W$.
  loop
    {In parallel on clients $\{c_i\}_{i=1}^W$}
    Download Σ_{t-1}, calculate current $\theta_{t-1} = \theta_0 + A(\Sigma_{t-1})$.
    Compute stochastic gradient g_i^t on batch B_i of size ℓ: $g_i^t = \frac{1}{\ell} \sum_{j=1}^{\ell} \nabla_\theta \mathcal{L}(\theta_{t-1}, z_j)$.
    Sketch g_i^t to $S_i^t = A^\top g_i^t$ and upload it to the aggregator.
  end loop
  Aggregate sketches $S^t = \frac{1}{W} \sum_{i=1}^W S_i^t$
  Unsketch: $\Delta_t = AS^t$
  Update: $\theta_t = \theta_{t-1} - \eta \Delta_t$, $\Sigma_t = \Sigma_{t-1} - \eta S^t$.
end for

namely that given by the span of A_t. This family of algorithms can be made to use only d upload bandwidth, as only the vector $A_t^\top(\boldsymbol{v}_t)$ must be uploaded. Furthermore, note that Equation (6) has no references to the intrinsic weights θ', meaning that it represents a general optimization algorithm in the original space. Formally,

Theorem 3.1. *All algorithms of the form*

$$\theta_{t+1} = \theta_t - \eta A_t A_t^\top (\boldsymbol{v}_t)$$

can be simulated with d upload bandwidth in a standard federated learning setting, where $\boldsymbol{v}_t$ is a function that can be calculated by the client at time t combined with all data from the server.

We call all such algorithms *intrinsic gradient compression algorithms*. Note that this theorem only bounds the upload bandwidth capacity needed to run gradient descent, and does not bound the download bandwidth. In the particular instantiations we consider, we will demonstrate that one can also bound the download bandwidth.

4 Intrinsic Gradient Compression Algorithms

While Theorem 3.1 shows that any algorithm of the form Equation (6) can be implemented with low levels of upload bandwidth, not every algorithm of the form Equation (6) can be implemented with low levels of download bandwidth as well. Theorem 3.1 gives rise to a family of algorithms we denote *intrinsic gradient compression algorithms*. In this section, we describe three particular intrinsic gradient compression algorithms which use low amounts of both upload and download bandwidth.

These federated learning algorithms can be decomposed into three main phases.

- **Reconciliation:** The client reconciles its model with the server's copy of the model.
- **Compression:** The local model calculates, compresses, and sends its local gradient to the server.
- **Decompression:** The server model updates its own copy of the model using the estimated gradient from the local model.

In general, reconciliation will be by far the most complex part of each algorithm, and the other steps are essentially shared across algorithms.

We show how to implement SGD for each variant, and note that this choice of optimization algorithm is quite necessary – other optimization algorithms like SGD with momentum cause the parameters to not move in the low-dimensional subspace, which makes the compression impossible. While one can implement a variant which resets the momentum every epoch, momentum is rarely a useful optimization in federated learning due to the non-i.i.d. nature of the batches) so we do not consider this.

Static Intrinsic Gradient Compression In this subsection, we seek to implement the static intrinsic gradient compression algorithm

$$\theta_t = \theta_{t-1} - \eta A A^\top \nabla_\theta \mathcal{L}(\theta_{t-1})$$

in a federated learning setting.

In the reconciliation phase, since we know that the parameters θ^c (which denotes the current parameters of the server) will always be equal to $\theta_0 + A\Sigma$ for some $\Sigma \in \mathbb{R}^d$, the server can just send Σ to the client, which will take d download bandwidth.

For compression, the client compresses the gradient by multiplying by $A^\top$, and for decompression the server multiplies this by A. The full algorithm is given in Algorithm 1.

Time-Varying Intrinsic Gradient Compression In this subsection, we implement the time-varying intrinsic gradient compression algorithm

$$\theta_t = \theta_{t-1} - \eta A_e A_e^\top \nabla_\theta \mathcal{L}(\theta_{t-1})$$

in a federated learning setting, where e is the epoch.

In this case, we show that our algorithm can be implemented with at most $2d$ bandwidth used per

Intrinsic Gradient Compression Method	Upload	Download	Dimensions Explored
Static	dE	dE	d
Time-Varying	dE	$2dE$	dE
K-Varying	dE	$2dEK$	dEK
No Compression	DE	DE	D

Table 1: Bandwidth and Performance Comparisons. The bandwidth refers to that of that used for each client. Note that we break upload and download bandwidth into separate columns, because download speeds can often be considerably faster than upload speeds and we may thus be willing to tolerate higher values of download bandwidth. A realistic example of the values of the variables above is e.g. $d = 10^3, D = 10^8, E = 20, K = 8$.

client per timestep, so over E epochs there is $2dE$ bandwidth used total on downloading. Since this bandwidth is twice that of static subspace compression, but we search E times more directions in the space, this algorithm is particularly useful when we have many epochs.

Letting θ_e^c be the client parameters at epoch e, note that we have the value of θ_{e-1}^c when performing reconciliation. Now we can write

$$\theta_e^c - \theta_{e-1}^c = (\theta_e^c - \theta_{e-1}^{\text{final}}) + (\theta_{e-1}^{\text{final}} - \theta_{e-1}^c)$$

and we can see that $(\theta_e^c - \theta_{e-1}^{\text{final}})$ lies in the column space of A_e and $(\theta_{e-1}^{\text{final}} - \theta_{e-1}^c)$ lies in the column space of A_{e-1}, which is enough to find the full algorithm, given in Algorithm 2.

K-Varying Intrinsic Gradient Compression In this subsection, we describe how to implement the K-varying intrinsic gradient compression algorithm

$$\theta_t = \theta_{t-1} - \eta A_e^{(i)} A_e^{(i)\top} \nabla_\theta \mathcal{L}(\theta_{t-1})$$

where $\{A_e^{(i)}\}_{i=1}^K$ is the set of K compression matrices used at epoch e, and i is a randomly chosen integer between 1 and K inclusive.

This method is motivated from the fact that in many cases, the upload speed is much slower than the download speed, so we may only want to project the gradient into part of the subspace currently being explored, as opposed to the complete subspace. This allows each client to explore d directions at a time, but for dK directions to be explored across the entire epoch. As such, the algorithm identical time-varying compression, and is given in Algorithm 3.

Choice of Compression Matrix Finally, we we discuss the choice of compression matrix for A. We note that our methods are agnostic to the specific choice of A, and depend only on the existence of efficient subroutines for calculating the matrix-vector products Ax and $A^\top y$. Nonetheless, the choice of A has significant implications for the resulting accuracy of the algorithms. In order to maintain the most proximity to the original stochastic gradient descent algorithm, we will choose normalized A so that $\mathbb{E}[AA^\top] = I_D$.

The naive choice is to let A be a $D \times d$ random dense matrix, but such a choice is impossible due to memory constraints. For example, if we aim to train even a small version of BERT (100M parameters) with an intrinsic dimension of 1000, we would need to store a matrix with 10^{11} entries.

The approach taken by (Aghajanyan et al., 2021; Li et al., 2018) for large-scale experiments, which we follow, utilizes the *Fastfood transform* (Le et al., 2013), in which A can be expressed as the $D \times d$ matrix $A_i = \text{Unpad}_D B_i H \Pi_i G_i H \text{Pad}_{2^\ell}$ where 2^ℓ is the smallest power of two larger than D, H is a standard Hadamard matrix, B_i is a random diagonal matrix with independent Rademacher entries (random signs), Π is a random permutation matrix, G is a random diagonal matrix with independent standard normal entries, Pad_{2^ℓ} to be a linear operator which simply pads a d-dimensional vector v with zeroes until it has size 2^ℓ, and Unpad_D is a linear operator which takes the first D elements from a 2^ℓ-dimensional vector. Since we can quickly compute a matrix-vector product by H with a fast Walsh-Hadamard transform, we can perform a matrix multiplication by $A_i A_i^\top$ in $O(\ell 2^\ell) = O(D \log D)$ time and $O(D)$ space.

Performance Comparison We show the theoretical tradeoffs between each of these algorithms in Table 1.

	Name	Intrinsic Dim.	PPL	Up. Comp.	Down. Comp.	Total Comp.
	Uncompressed		13.9	1	1	1
(McMahan et al., 2017)	FedAvg (2 local iters)		16.3	2	2	2
(McMahan et al., 2017)	FedAvg (5 local iters)		20.1	5	5	5
	Local Top-K ($k = 50,000$)		19.3	30.3	2490	60
	Local Top-K ($k = 500,000$)		17.1	3.6	248	7.1
(Rothchild et al., 2020)	FetchSGD ($k = 25,000$)		**14.8**	3.8	100	7.3
(Rothchild et al., 2020)	FetchSGD ($k = 50,000$)		15.8	2.4	10	3.9
	Ours (static)	16384	27.7	7595	7595	7595
	Ours (K-subspace)	16384	19.6	7595	949	1688
	Ours (static)	65536	20.6	1900	1900	1900
	Ours (K-subspace)	65536	17.8	1900	237	422
	Ours (static)	262144	17.6	475	475	475
	Ours (K-subspace)	262144	16.6	475	59.3	105
	Ours (static)	1048576	15.8	119	119	119
	Ours (K-subspace)	1048576	15.4	119	14.8	26.3
	Ours (static)	4194304	**14.8**	29.7	29.7	29.7

Table 2: Language modeling perplexity (lower is better) and compression rates (higher is better) for a GPT-2 model (124M parameters) on the PersonaChat dataset. We compare to prior work, including the state-of-the-art in gradient compression (FetchSGD), and we show upload, download, and total compression rates. For our intrinsic gradient compression results, we give static and K-subspace compression for a range of dimensions between 16386 and 4194304. For K-subspace compression we use $K = 8$. Overall, we match or exceed the performance of prior work with significantly improved compression rates.

5 Experiments

We evaluate our method across a range of benchmarks to showcase the potential of our three algorithms. These include two natural language processing tasks (language modeling and text classification), as well as a computer vision task (image classification).

As with previous works (Rothchild et al., 2020; McMahan et al., 2017), we simulate the federated learning in order to scale to large numbers of clients (upwards of $10,000$). We simulate on 8 commercial-grade GPUs for the language modeling experiments and 1 GPU for the other experiments. We perform experiments in both non-IID (language modeling, image classification) and IID (text classification) settings, because both scenarios are common in real-world federated learning.

Image Classification (ResNet-9 on CIFAR-10) First, we consider image classification on the CIFAR-10 dataset, a collection of 50,000 images with resolution 32×32px. We use the same experimental setup as (Rothchild et al., 2020): we split the data between 10,000 clients in a non-IID fashion, such that each client only has data from a single class. At each step, we sample 100 clients at random, such that each gradient step corresponds to 500 images. We perform 24 rounds of communication between all clients (i.e. 24 training epochs).

We use a ResNet-9 architecture with 6,570,880 trainable parameters for our fair comparison to previous work. Note that the model does not have batch normalization, as batch normalization would not make sense in a setting where each client has so few examples. Due to the substantial number of epochs performed here, we experiment with both static and time-varying gradient compression (k-varying compression is better suited to settings involving fewer rounds of communication). We perform experiments across intrinsic dimensions of 4000, 8000, 16000, 32000, 64000, 128000, and 256000.

Our results are shown in Figure 1. Whereas FedAvg and Top-K struggle at even modest compression rates (e.g. $3\times$), the intrinsic gradient compression methods deliver strong performance at much larger compression rates. The intrinsic methods outperform the current state-of-the-art gradient compression method, FetchSGD (Rothchild et al., 2020), by a large margin, and easily scale to high compression rates (e.g. $100\times$). Finally, we see that time-varying intrinsic compression generally outperforms static compression for the same communication cost.

Text Classification (BERT on SST-2) Next, we consider text classification on the Stanford Senti-

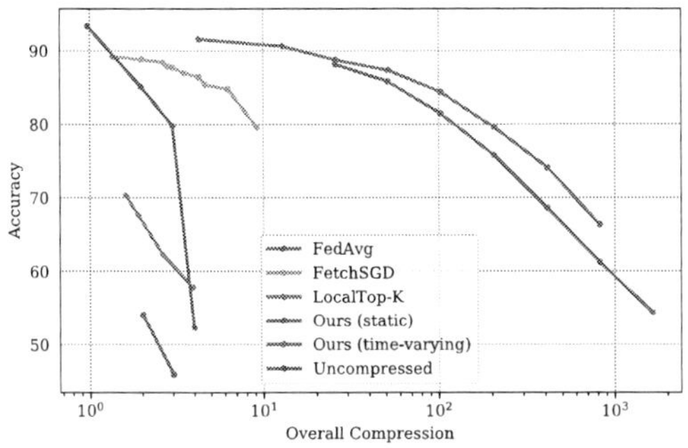

(a) Final Accuracies on CIFAR-10 with differing levels of compression.

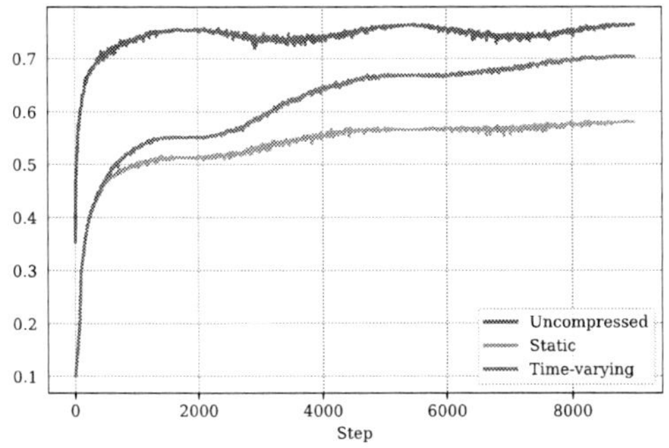

(b) Training curves on CIFAR-10 with static and time varying dimension at the same intrinsic dimensionality.

Figure 1: Results on computer vision benchmarks. Both static and time-varying intrinsic gradient dimension significantly outperform perform work, with time-varying intrinsic compression performing best. On the right, we see that time-varying and static compression perform similarly at the beginning of training, but time-varying outperforms static eventually but are tied at the beginning, and that time-varying outperforms static with equal space. For the FedAvg and uncompressed methods with compression rates above 1, compression was performed by training for fewer epochs.

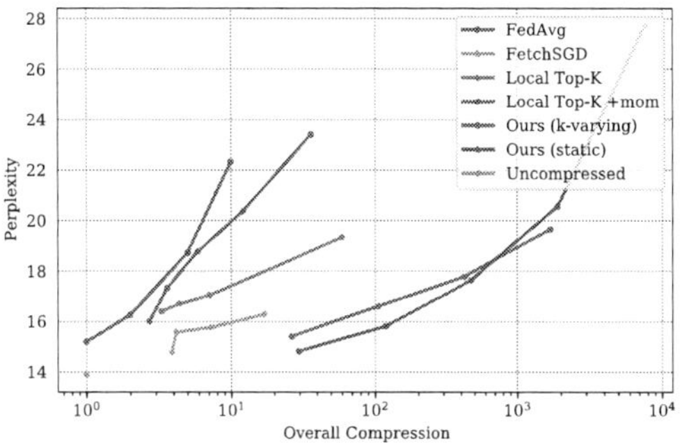

(a) Perplexity on PersonaChat compared to other recent federated learning methods

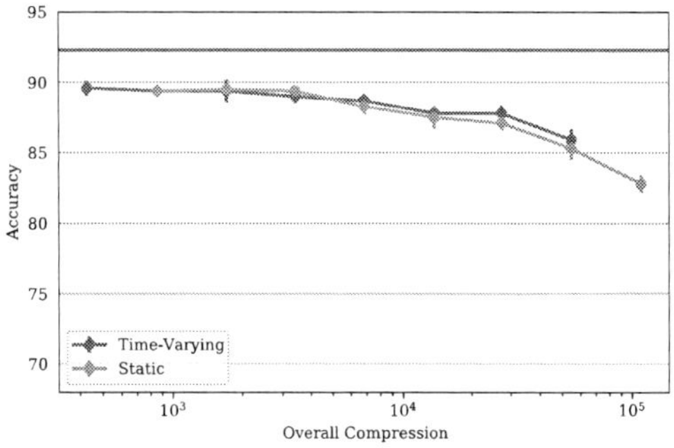

(b) Accuracy on SST-2

Figure 2: Results on NLP benchmarks. Note that while K-varying appears to perform poorly on PersonaChat, the upload performance is much stronger. See Appendix D for these full results.

ment Treebank-v2 (SST-2) dataset (Socher et al., 2013), a common sentiment analysis dataset. For this experiment, we consider an IID data split into 50 and 500 clients, respectively. We employ the popular BERT (Devlin et al., 2019) transformer architecture with 109M parameters. The purpose of this experiment is to push the limits of gradient compression; we project the 109M-dimension BERT gradients into as few as 200 dimensions.

We perform 30 rounds (i.e. 30 epochs) of training for all compressed runs, while we perform 6 for the uncompressed baseline (as it converges more quickly). Federated learning experiments has previously been criticized for being challenging to reproduce; as a result, we perform each run five times over different random seeds. We report the mean, min, max, and standard deviation of the runs in Appendix D.

Due to the substantial number of epochs performed here, it is natural to apply static and time-varying intrinsic gradient compression. We use intrinsic dimensions of 200, 400, 800, . . . , 25600.

Our results are given in Figure 2. First, along similar lines to (Aghajanyan et al., 2021), we find that it is possible to achieve remarkably high compression ratios for text classification: we achieve close to full performance even when compressing the 109M-dimension parameter vector into an intrinsic space of dimension 16,384. Furthermore, we find that time-varying intrinsic gradient compression consistently outperforms static intrinsic gradient compression at the same compression rate.

Language Modeling (GPT-2 on PersonaChat) Lastly, we consider language modeling on the PersonaChat (Zhang et al., 2018) dataset of dialogues between Amazon Mechanical Turk workers assigned to act out specific personalities. [1] The dataset has a non-IID split into 17,568 clients in which each client is assigned all data corresponding to given personality; as a result, it is widely used in federated learning simulations. We perform language modeling using the GPT-2 transformer architecture (124M parameters). For fair comparison to previous work, we conduct only two rounds of training across the clients (i.e. two epochs).

Due to the low number of training rounds, it is natural to apply *static* and *K-varying* gradient compression.[2] Specifically, we apply both of these algorithms to train GPT-2 using intrinsic dimensions of 16384, 65536, 262144, 1048576, and 4194304.

Our results are shown in Figure 2. Overall, intrinsic dimension-based gradient compression vastly outperforms a wide range of prior approaches to reducing communication in federated learning. On the low-compression end of the spectrum, we obtain nearly full performance with superior compression rates to FedAvg (McMahan et al., 2017) and the recent FetchSGD (Rothchild et al., 2020). On the high-compression end of the spectrum, we scale better than previous approaches. For example, we obtain a perplexity of around 20 even with an extremely high compression rate of 1898.

Finally, we see that K-varying intrinsic compression performs similarly to (or slightly worse) than static compression at the same level of overall compression. However, if it is more important to conserve upload bandwidth than download bandwidth, then K-varying intrinsic gradient compression significantly outperforms static intrinsic gradient compression (see Section 4).

5.1 Gradient Compression Results

One of the primary motivations of federated learning is the desire for individual clients to be able to retain data privacy while still participating in model training.

However, a number of works have shown that if the client does not have a large amount of data and the client sends back their full local gradient, it is possible to approximately reconstruct their local data from the model. This is a significant problem, because their data would then effectively be visible to the central server and any attackers that intercept their communications.

Here, we show that compressing gradients with our approach can mitigate this problem. Specifically, we check if our compressed gradients can be reconstructed with the procedure proposed by (Zhu et al., 2019). As in (Zhu et al., 2019), we use a ResNet-152 model a randomly selected image from ImageNet and run for 24,000 iterations (by which time the method has converged). We reconstruct the image both from the full gradient (the center image) and from a the intrinsically-compressed image (the right image) with intrinsic dimension 65,536.

As seen in Figure 3, given the full gradient it is possible to obtain a fairly good reconstruction of the image. By contrast, with our method, the reconstruction is visually much less similar from original image. Of course, our method does not solve the problem entirely; an outline of the dog in the image is still visible because the compressed gradient still contains some information about the local data. To solve the issue entirely, it would be necessary to use a method such as differential privacy.

6 Conclusion

Federated learning holds the promise of large-scale model training while simultaneously letting users retain control over their data. In this paper, we preset a set of novel algorithms for scalable and efficient federated learning. These algorithms are particularly helpful for NLP training, where models often have hundreds of millions of parameters. Our experiments finetuning BERT and GPT-2 that our proposed method significantly improves upon the state-of-the-art in gradient compression for federated learning. In future work, we hope to deploy our system in a real-world federated learning setting with a large number of physical devices, rather than solely in simulation.

7 Acknowledgments

We would like to thank Ankur Moitra, Yang Liu, and Demi Guo for helpful discussions. L. M. K. is supported by the Rhodes Trust.

[1] In more detail, the PersonaChat dataset (Zhang et al., 2018) was collected by first giving imaginary personas (defined by a set of 5 sentences) to Amazon Mechanical Turk workers and asking them to take on those personas. Then, the system paired workers and asked them to discuss. Since the personas were imaginary and no personally identifiable information was exchanged (in particular, the workers were explicitly told to not use personally identifiable information) the dataset does not contain personally identifiable information.

[2] Time-varying compression does not make sense here, as its benefit is derived from the setting where there are many rounds of communication between the clients.

References

Armen Aghajanyan, Sonal Gupta, and Luke Zettlemoyer. 2021. Intrinsic dimensionality explains the effectiveness of language model fine-tuning. In *Proceedings of the 59th Annual Meeting of the Association for Computational Linguistics and the 11th International Joint Conference on Natural Language Processing, ACL/IJCNLP 2021, (Volume 1: Long Papers), Virtual Event, August 1-6, 2021*, pages 7319–7328. Association for Computational Linguistics.

Alyazeed Albasyoni, Mher Safaryan, Laurent Condat, and Peter Richtárik. 2020. Optimal gradient compression for distributed and federated learning. *arXiv preprint arXiv:2010.03246*.

Arjun Nitin Bhagoji, Supriyo Chakraborty, Prateek Mittal, and Seraphin Calo. 2019. Analyzing federated learning through an adversarial lens. In *International Conference on Machine Learning*, pages 634–643. PMLR.

Sameer Bibikar, Haris Vikalo, Zhangyang Wang, and Xiaohan Chen. 2021. Federated dynamic sparse training: Computing less, communicating less, yet learning better. *arXiv preprint arXiv:2112.09824*.

Claudio Ceruti, Simone Bassis, Alessandro Rozza, Gabriele Lombardi, Elena Casiraghi, and Paola Campadelli. 2014. Danco: An intrinsic dimensionality estimator exploiting angle and norm concentration. *Pattern Recognition*, 47(8):2569–2581.

Jacob Devlin, Ming-Wei Chang, Kenton Lee, and Kristina Toutanova. 2019. BERT: Pre-training of deep bidirectional transformers for language understanding. In *Proceedings of the 2019 Conference of the North American Chapter of the Association for Computational Linguistics: Human Language Technologies, Volume 1 (Long and Short Papers)*, pages 4171–4186, Minneapolis, Minnesota. Association for Computational Linguistics.

Sixue Gong, Vishnu Naresh Boddeti, and Anil K Jain. 2019. On the intrinsic dimensionality of image representations. In *Proceedings of the IEEE/CVF Conference on Computer Vision and Pattern Recognition*, pages 3987–3996.

Demi Guo, Alexander M Rush, and Yoon Kim. 2021. Parameter-efficient transfer learning with diff pruning. In *ACL*.

P. Han, S. Wang, and K. K. Leung. 2020. Adaptive gradient sparsification for efficient federated learning: An online learning approach. In *2020 IEEE 40th International Conference on Distributed Computing Systems (ICDCS)*, pages 300–310, Los Alamitos, CA, USA. IEEE Computer Society.

Song Han, Huizi Mao, and William J Dally. 2015. Deep compression: Compressing deep neural networks with pruning, trained quantization and huffman coding. *arXiv preprint arXiv:1510.00149*.

Chaoyang He, Songze Li, Jinhyun So, Mi Zhang, Hongyi Wang, Xiaoyang Wang, Praneeth Vepakomma, Abhishek Singh, Hang Qiu, Li Shen, Peilin Zhao, Yan Kang, Yang Liu, Ramesh Raskar, Qiang Yang, Murali Annavaram, and Salman Avestimehr. 2020. Fedml: A research library and benchmark for federated machine learning. *arXiv preprint arXiv:2007.13518*.

Geoffrey Hinton, Oriol Vinyals, and Jeff Dean. 2015. Distilling the knowledge in a neural network. *arXiv preprint arXiv:1503.02531*.

Neil Houlsby, Andrei Giurgiu, Stanislaw Jastrzebski, Bruna Morrone, Quentin De Laroussilhe, Andrea Gesmundo, Mona Attariyan, and Sylvain Gelly. 2019. Parameter-efficient transfer learning for NLP. In *Proceedings of the 36th International Conference on Machine Learning*.

Yuang Jiang, Shiqiang Wang, Victor Valls, Bong Jun Ko, Wei-Han Lee, Kin K Leung, and Leandros Tassiulas. 2019. Model pruning enables efficient federated learning on edge devices. *arXiv preprint arXiv:1909.12326*.

Quoc V. Le, Tamás Sarlós, and Alexander J. Smola. 2013. Fastfood - computing hilbert space expansions in loglinear time. In *Proceedings of the 30th International Conference on Machine Learning, ICML 2013, Atlanta, GA, USA, 16-21 June 2013*, volume 28 of *JMLR Workshop and Conference Proceedings*, pages 244–252. JMLR.org.

Elizaveta Levina and Peter Bickel. 2005. Maximum likelihood estimation of intrinsic dimension. In *Advances in Neural Information Processing Systems*, volume 17. MIT Press.

Chunyuan Li, Heerad Farkhoor, Rosanne Liu, and Jason Yosinski. 2018. Measuring the intrinsic dimension of objective landscapes. In *International Conference on Learning Representations*.

Tian Li, Anit Kumar Sahu, Manzil Zaheer, Maziar Sanjabi, Ameet Talwalkar, and Virginia Smith. 2020a. Federated optimization in heterogeneous networks. In *ML Sys*.

Xiang Li, Kaixuan Huang, Wenhao Yang, Shusen Wang, and Zhihua Zhang. 2020b. On the convergence of fedavg on non-iid data. In *International Conference on Learning Representations*.

Zhize Li, Dmitry Kovalev, Xun Qian, and Peter Richtarik. 2020c. Acceleration for compressed gradient descent in distributed and federated optimization. In *Proceedings of the 37th International Conference on Machine Learning*, volume 119 of *Proceedings of Machine Learning Research*, pages 5895–5904. PMLR.

Grigory Malinovsky, Dmitry Kovalev, Elnur Gasanov, Laurent Condat, and Peter Richtárik. 2020. From local sgd to local fixed-point methods for federated learning. In *ICML*.

Brendan McMahan, Eider Moore, Daniel Ramage, Seth Hampson, and Blaise Aguera y Arcas. 2017. Communication-efficient learning of deep networks from decentralized data. In *Artificial Intelligence and Statistics*, pages 1273–1282. PMLR.

Mehryar Mohri, Gary Sivek, and Ananda Theertha Suresh. 2019. Agnostic federated learning. In *International Conference on Machine Learning*, pages 4615–4625. PMLR.

Phil Pope, Chen Zhu, Ahmed Abdelkader, Micah Goldblum, and Tom Goldstein. 2021. The intrinsic dimension of images and its impact on learning. In *International Conference on Learning Representations*.

Elad Ravfogel, Shauli Ben-Zaken, and Yoav Goldberg. 2021. Bitfit: Simple parameter-efficient fine-tuning for transformer-based masked language-models. *arXiv preprint*.

Sashank J. Reddi, Zachary Charles, Manzil Zaheer, Zachary Garrett, Keith Rush, Jakub Konečný, Sanjiv Kumar, and Hugh Brendan McMahan. 2021. Adaptive federated optimization. In *International Conference on Learning Representations*.

Daniel Rothchild, Ashwinee Panda, Enayat Ullah, Nikita Ivkin, Ion Stoica, Vladimir Braverman, Joseph Gonzalez, and Raman Arora. 2020. Fetchsgd: Communication-efficient federated learning with sketching. In *Proceedings of the 37th International Conference on Machine Learning, ICML 2020, 13-18 July 2020, Virtual Event*, volume 119 of *Proceedings of Machine Learning Research*, pages 8253–8265. PMLR.

Richard Socher, Alex Perelygin, Jean Wu, Jason Chuang, Christopher D Manning, Andrew Y Ng, and Christopher Potts. 2013. Recursive deep models for semantic compositionality over a sentiment treebank. In *Proceedings of the 2013 conference on empirical methods in natural language processing*, pages 1631–1642.

Yue Tan, Guodong Long, Lu Liu, Tianyi Zhou, and Jing Jiang. 2021. Fedproto: Federated prototype learning over heterogeneous devices. *arXiv preprint arXiv:2105.00243*.

Hongyi Wang, Mikhail Yurochkin, Yuekai Sun, Dimitris Papailiopoulos, and Yasaman Khazaeni. 2020. Federated learning with matched averaging. In *International Conference on Learning Representations*.

Wei Wen, Cong Xu, Feng Yan, Chunpeng Wu, Yandan Wang, Yiran Chen, and Hai Li. 2017. Terngrad: Ternary gradients to reduce communication in distributed deep learning. In *Advances in Neural Information Processing Systems 30: Annual Conference on Neural Information Processing Systems 2017, December 4-9, 2017, Long Beach, CA, USA*, pages 1509–1519.

Chulin Xie, Keli Huang, Pin-Yu Chen, and Bo Li. 2020. Dba: Distributed backdoor attacks against federated learning. In *International Conference on Learning Representations*.

Felix X. Yu, Ankit Singh Rawat, Aditya Krishna Menon, and Sanjiv Kumar. 2020. Federated learning with only positive labels.

Saizheng Zhang, Emily Dinan, Jack Urbanek, Arthur Szlam, Douwe Kiela, and Jason Weston. 2018. Personalizing dialogue agents: I have a dog, do you have pets too? In *Proceedings of the 56th Annual Meeting of the Association for Computational guistics (Volume 1: Long Papers)*, pages 2204–2213.

Ligeng Zhu, Zhijian Liu, and Song Han. 2019. Deep leakage from gradients. In *Advances in Neural Information Processing Systems 32: Annual Conference on Neural Information Processing Systems 2019, NeurIPS 2019, December 8-14, 2019, Vancouver, BC, Canada*, pages 14747–14756.

Appendix

A Algorithms

In Algorithm 2 and Algorithm 3 below, we provide the full time-varying and K-varying intrinsic gradient compression algorithms, which were omitted from the main text.

B Proofs

B.1 Proof of Theorem 3.1

First, note that the server knows the value of A_t. Then, for any local vector $\boldsymbol{v}_t$, the client can send $A_t^\top(\boldsymbol{v}_t)$ to the server, and the server can calculate $A_t A_t^\top$, enabling it to continue executing the algorithm.

C Additional Related work

In the main paper, we described the prior work in federated learning and machine learning theory that was directly relevant to our paper's method. Here, we describe a number of less-related works that could not be included in the main paper due to space constraints.

Intrinsic Dimensionality As mentioned in the main paper, the concept of measuring the intrinsic dimensional of loss landscapes was introduced by (Li et al., 2018). (Li et al., 2018) consider optimizing a D-parameter model in a random d-dimensional subspace of the full parameter space. They define the intrinsic dimension of the optimization problem as the minimum dimension d for which a solution to the problem can be found, where a "solution" refers attaining a certain percentage of the maximum possible validation accuracy (i.e. the validation accuracy obtained by optimizing in all D dimensions). They use a fixed cut-off of 90% accuracy for their experiments.

(Aghajanyan et al., 2021) followed up on this work by considering the setting of finetuning models in natural language processing. They show that the intrinsic dimension of some of these tasks (e.g. text classification on MRPC) is surprisingly low.

A number of works have tried to measure the intrinsic dimension of datasets, rather than objective landscapes. (Levina and Bickel, 2005) introduced a maximum likelihood approach to estimating intrinsic dimensionality based on nearest-neighbors, while (Ceruti et al., 2014) employed angle and norm-based similarity. More recently, () further extended this line of work to use minimal neighborhood information.

Finally, some works have tried to measure the intrinsic dimensionality of image representations and datasets. (Gong et al., 2019) finds that the representations produced by popular image and face representation learning models (ResNet-50 and SphereFace) have quite low intrinsic dimensionalities (16 and 19, respectively). Along similar lines, (Pope et al., 2021) showed that popular image datasets (MNIST, CIFAR 10, ImageNet) also have low intrinsic dimensionality.

Federated Learning Federated learning is generally concerned with the distributed training of machine learning models across many devices, each of which holds private data. Many aspects of this federated setup are separate subfields of research, including how to ensure the privacy of client-held data (Xie et al., 2020; Bhagoji et al., 2019), how to deal with heterogeneous data and networks (Li et al., 2020a,b; Yu et al., 2020), how to reconcile weights/gradients from multiple clients (Li et al., 2020a; Wang et al., 2020; Li et al., 2020c), how to manage clients in a fault-tolerant manner, deployment on mobile/iot devices (He et al., 2020), and fairness (Mohri et al., 2019).

Numerous works focus on making federated training more efficient, with the ultimate goal of reducing communication cost and training time. The classic FedAvg (McMahan et al., 2017) algorithm tries to do this by communicating weights rather than gradients. FedProx (Li et al., 2020a) generalizes and re-parametrizes FedAvg. FedMA (Wang et al., 2020) continues to improve this approach by matching and averaging hidden layers of networks with similar activations at each communication round. FedAwS (Yu et al., 2020) considers federated averaging in the case where each client has data from only a single class. (Malinovsky et al., 2020) analyzes a generalization of these weight-averaging approaches from a theoretical viewpoint.

Relative to the weight averaging approach, the approach of compressing and sending gradients is relatively understudied. (Albasyoni et al., 2020) describes an approach that is theoretically optimal but not practical for large non-linear models. (Han et al., 2020) proposes adaptive gradient sparsification for federated learning, in which a subset of the full gradient is communicated at each round. FetchSGD (Rothchild et al., 2020) compresses gradients by sketching; it is the current state-of-the-art

Algorithm 2 Time-Varying Intrinsic Gradient Compression

input: learning rate η, timesteps T, local batch size ℓ, clients per round W
for $e = 1, 2, \cdots E$ **do**
  Create matrix $A_e \overset{\text{i.i.d.}}{\sim} A$ where $A \in \mathbb{R}^{D \times d}$ with $\mathbb{E}[AA^\top] = I_D$.
  Current, Final Vector: $\Sigma_e^{\text{current}} = 0$, $\Sigma_e^{\text{final}} = 0$
  for $t = 1, 2 \cdots T$ **do**
    Randomly select W clients $c_1, \ldots c_W$.
    loop
      {In parallel on clients $\{c_i\}_{i=1}^W$}
      Download $\Sigma_e^{\text{current}}$, $\Sigma_{e-1}^{\text{final}}$, calculate current $\theta_e^{c_i} = \theta_{e-1}^{c_i} + A_{e-1}(\Sigma_{e-1}^{\text{final}} - \Sigma^{\text{last}}) + A_e(\Sigma_e^{\text{current}})$.
      Update $\Sigma^{\text{last}} = \Sigma_e^{\text{current}}$.
      Compute stochastic gradient g_i^t on batch B_i of size ℓ: $g_i^t = \frac{1}{\ell}\sum_{j=1}^{\ell} \nabla_\theta \mathcal{L}(\theta_e^{c_i}, z_j)$.
      Sketch g_i^t : $S_i^{(e)t} = A_e^\top g_i^t$ and upload it to the aggregator.
    end loop
    Aggregate sketches $S^{(e)t} = \frac{1}{W}\sum_{i=1}^{W} S_i^{(e)t}$
    Unsketch: $\Delta^{(e)t} = A_e S^{(e)t}$
    Update: $\theta^{\text{current}} = \theta^{\text{current}} - \eta\Delta^{(e)t}$, $\Sigma_e^{\text{current}} = \Sigma_e^{\text{current}} - \eta S^{(e)t}$.
  end for
  Let $\Sigma_e^{\text{final}} = \Sigma_e^{\text{current}}$.
end for

in gradient compression for federated learning. We describe it in further depth in the main paper.

Finally, (Reddi et al., 2021) and (Li et al., 2020c) accelerate training by bringing adaptive optimizers built for centralized learning into the federated setting.

D Further Experimental Analysis

In the main paper, we included a number of figures demonstrating our performance in comparison to prior work. Here, we include tables with our precise results for clarity and in order to facilitate future comparison with our work.

D.1 Further PersonaChat Analysis

Section 4 shows full results on PersonaChat, complete with upload and download compression. Overall compression is calculated as average compression over both upload and download.

We compare with FedAvg (McMahan et al., 2017), Top-K, and FetchSGD (Rothchild et al., 2020). FedAvg is the baseline federated learning approach involving sending and averaging weights. Top-K refers to sending the top gradients, sorted by magnitude. FetchSGD compresses the weights with sketching.

Our method significantly outperforms competing approaches across the board. We obtain an accuracy close to that of uncompressed optimization using INSERTx overall compression; FedAvg and Top-K both fail to achieve such strong results, while FetchSGD does so at a significantly lower compression rate.

Next we compare static and K-varying intrinsic gradient compression. When comparing overall compression rates, static compression is slightly better than K-varying compression. However, K-varying compression is optimized for low upload bandwidth; it obtains much better upload compression rates than static compression at the same accuracy. For example, K-varying compression with $k = 8$ and $d = 65536$ yields perplexity 17.6 at upload compression 1900×, whereas static compression with $d = 262144$ yields perplexity 17.4 at upload compression 475×.

D.2 Further SST-2 Analysis

In Table 3, we show full results for the SST-2 dataset with static and time-varying gradient compression for a range of intrinsic dimensions. We include in this experiment an demonstration of the robustness of our method to variation in random seeds; we run each experiment five times using separate random seeds (i.e. different intrinsic subspaces and model initializations). We report standard errors in Table 3; variability is quite low.

We also see that time-varying intrinsic gradient compression outperforms static intrinsic compression, especially for low intrinsic dimensions. For example, time-varying compression at $d = 200$ outperforms static compression with $d = 400$, and time-varying compression with $d = 400$ outperforms static compression with $d = 800$.

Algorithm 3 K-Varying Intrinsic Gradient Compression

input: distinct subspaces K, learning rate η, timesteps T, local batch size ℓ, clients per round W
for $e = 1, 2, \ldots E$ **do**
  Create matrices $A_e^{(1)}, A_e^{(2)}, \ldots A_e^{(K)} \overset{\text{i.i.d.}}{\sim} A$ where $A \in \mathbb{R}^{D \times d}$ with $\mathbb{E}[AA^\top] = I_D$.
  Current, Final Vector: $\Sigma_e^{\text{current}(k)} = 0$, $\Sigma_e^{\text{final}(k)} = 0$ for $k = 1, 2, \ldots K$.
  for $t = 1, 2 \cdots T$ **do**
    Randomly select W clients $c_1, \ldots c_W$.
    loop
      {In parallel on clients $\{c_i\}_{i=1}^W$}
      Download $\Sigma_e^{\text{current}(k)}$, $\Sigma_{e-1}^{\text{final}(k)}$ for $k = 1, \ldots K$, and calculate:
        $\theta_e^{c_i} = \theta_{e-1}^{c_i} + \sum_{k=1}^K \left(A_{e-1}(\Sigma_{e-1}^{\text{final}(k)} - \Sigma^{\text{last}(k)}) + A_e(\Sigma_e^{\text{current}(k)}). \right)$
        $\Sigma^{\text{last}(k)} = \Sigma_e^{c(k)}$ for $k = 1, 2, \ldots K$.
      Choose a random $k_1 \sim \text{DUnif}(\{1, 2, \ldots K\})$
      Compute stochastic gradient g_i^t on batch B_i of size ℓ: $g_i^t = \frac{1}{\ell} \sum_{j=1}^{\ell} \nabla_\theta \mathcal{L}(\theta_e^{c_i}, z_j)$.
      Sketch $g_i^t : S_i^{(e)t} = (k_1, A_e^{(k_1)\top} g_i^t)$ and upload it to the aggregator.
    end loop
    Write sketches received as $\{S_w^{(e)t}\}_{w=1}^W = \{(j_w, C_w^{(e)t})\}_{w=1}^W$.
    Unsketch $S^{(e)t}$ to get $\Delta^{(e)t} = \frac{1}{W} \sum_{w=1}^W A_e^{(j_w)} C_w^{(e)t}$
    Update: $\theta^{\text{current}} = \theta^{\text{current}} - \eta \Delta^{(e)t}$,
    for $k = 1, 2 \ldots K$ **do**
      Update: $\Sigma_e^{\text{current}(k)} = \Sigma_e^{\text{current}(k)} - \frac{\eta}{W} \sum_{w, j_w = k} C_w^{(e)t}$.
    end for
  end for
  Let $\Sigma_e^{\text{final}(k)} = \Sigma_e^{c(k)}$ for $k = 1, 2, \ldots K$.
end for

(a) Input (b) Reconstruction from full gradient. (c) Reconstruction from gradient with intrinsic compression.

Figure 3: Image reconstruction from gradients with and without our intrinsic gradient compression method. On the left, we show the original image. In the center, we show the result of reconstructing the image from a single gradient from a ResNet-152 model (60M parameters), produced using the method of (Zhu et al., 2019). On the right, we show the result of the same image reconstruction method applied to an gradient compressed by our algorithm using intrinsic dimension 65,536.

Intrinsic Dim.	200	400	800	1,600
Static	82.8 ($\pm$0.69)	85.3 ($\pm$0.89)	87.1 ($\pm$0.57)	87.5 ($\pm$0.94)
Time-Varying	85.9 ($\pm$0.85)	87.8 ($\pm$0.61)	87.8 ($\pm$0.59)	88.7 ($\pm$0.54)

Intrinsic Dim.	3,200	6,400	12,800	25,600
Static	88.3 ($\pm$0.65)	89.4 ($\pm$0.33)	89.5 ($\pm$0.21)	89.5 ($\pm$0.21)
Time-Varying	89.0 ($\pm$0.53)	89.4 ($\pm$0.91)	89.4 ($\pm$0.19)	89.4 ($\pm$0.19)

Table 3: Accuracy and standard error of a BERT model trained on the Stanford Sentiment Treebank v2 (SST-2) for varying intrinsic dimensions. We calculate the standard error over five trials with different random seeds. We see that for fixed dimension, time-varying intrinsic gradient compression outperforms static intrinsic gradient compression.

Author Index

Avestimehr, Salman, 1

Breiner, Theresa, 6

Chen, Huili, 1
Chen, Mingqing, 6

Ding, Jie, 1

Gong, li, 21

Kumar, Shankar, 6

Mathews, Rajiv, 6
McConnaughey, Lara, 6
Melas-Kyriazi, Luke, 27

Ro, Jae Hun, 6

Sahu, Anit Kumar, 1
Suresh, Ananda Theertha, 6

Tramel, Eric William, 1

Wang, Franklyn, 27
Wu, Shuang, 1
Wu, Xinwei, 21

Xiong, Deyi, 21

Zhang, Tao, 1